Wicked
LAWRENCE COUNTY,
Ohio

Wicked
LAWRENCE COUNTY,
Ohio

LORI SHAFER

THE
History
PRESS

Published by The History Press
Charleston, SC
www.historypress.com

First published 2024

Manufactured in the United States

ISBN 9781467157865

Library of Congress Control Number: 2024936956

Notice: The information in this book is true and complete to the best of our knowledge. It is offered without guarantee on the part of the author or The History Press. The author and The History Press disclaim all liability in connection with the use of this book.

I would like to dedicate my book to my family.
Without your help and support, I could not be the person I am
and pursue my passions.

CONTENTS

ACKNOWLEDGEMENTS

I could not have written this book without the amazing staff at Briggs Lawrence County Public Library. I need to give a special thanks to the Phyllis Hamner Local History and Genealogy Room's Jonda Morgan and Cindy Wilson. Your assistance has made this book possible.

1

RED LIGHTS OVER LAWRENCE COUNTY

Red lights once signaled the special section of town where men could find prostitutes selling their wares. In some cases, the phrase literally referred to red lights marking the houses or streets. In other cases, the phrase was just a euphemism for a section of a town, county, city and so on that residents did not want to recognize.

The red-light district in Ironton was the least-kept secret in the tristate area. Everyone who needed to know it knew where it was. Even local law enforcement knew where to find it. No one really liked to talk about it.

Not everyone referred to it as the red-light district; some other phrases were used to denote the local whorehouses. The phrase "sporting district" became popular in the late 1890s. The Lawrence County Jail Register refers to houses of ill fame, keeping a disorderly house, streetwalking, keeping house, keeping a bad house and prostitution. One person was even charged with indecent conduct on the street.

Regardless of what phrase was used, the world's oldest profession was alive and well in Ironton well into the mid-1900s.

Historical records can be few and far between for Lawrence County criminals. The courthouse's numerous fires can account for some of the lack of records. Some jail registries can be found covering 1867 to 1910.

David Severy can claim notoriety for being the first person in the jail register arrested for crimes associated with prostitution. David was arrested on April 7, 1871, for "keeping a disorderly house." He spent six days in jail for his crime and was released on April 13, 1871.

In 1877, Ironton's mayor claimed there were eighty-one prostitutes actively working within the city limits. Obviously, the mayor knew about the red-light district, but he did not mention any efforts to curtail illegal activity.

FRANCES SMITH

One of the more well-known madams was Frances Smith. Frances was born in April 1857, and her maiden name was McMaster. On October 26, 1887, Frances married Michael Smith in Lawrence County, Ohio. She first appeared in the jail register when she was arrested for intoxication on March 8, 1892. She served only one day before being released. Interestingly enough, her husband, Michael, was a bartender.

In August 1888, Frances gave birth to the first of four children she would have with Michael, a daughter named Katherine. She was followed by Mary M., born in October 1890; James M., born in December 1892; and Bernard S., born in March 1895.

Her domestic bliss did not last long after the birth of her last child. Frances would be arrested for the first time for prostitution just three years later. On May 24, 1895, she was arrested for "keeping house." She remained in custody for only one day. For her crimes, Frances was fined fifty dollars.

Just a few days over a year later, Frances was arrested once again. The cause for her arrest was not listed in the jail register. What happened to her was documented. Her husband and Ward Smith sent her to the Athens Insane Asylum.

Marriage license for Michael Smith and Frances McMaster. *Briggs Lawrence County Public Library, Hamner Room.*

Athens Insane Asylum. *Author's collection.*

Women could be sent to an asylum for a variety of reasons at this time in history. The Athens Asylum had ninety-two women admitted for the first time in 1895. Frances was one of them. Twenty-nine other women were readmitted. Of those admitted, fifty-nine recovered. The majority, sixty-five, were married, like Frances. Hereditary conditions and ill health were the most common physical causes for admissions, with twenty-one each. Domestic problems were the most common "moral" cause for admissions. Considering Frances's criminal history, one can assume she was admitted for domestic problems.

Frances may have ceased her illegal activities for a while, since she did not have any more arrests recorded for two years. But she was unable to resist returning to her life of crime. On April 28, 1898, Frances was arrested once again for keeping a house of ill fame. She was released two days later when she was able to pay her bond.

She would be arrested again on November 2, 1898. Once again, she was accused of operating a whorehouse. She was fined one hundred dollars and released.

After 1898, Frances seemed to stay on the straight and narrow. Either that or she was no longer getting caught. She and Michael owned the Cannon and Smith Saloon located at 121 North Third Street in Ironton. They made their home at 1004 North Fifth Street.

Sarah M. Halliday

A contemporary of Frances was Sarah M. Halliday. She was first arrested in early May 1898 for keeping a bad house. "Keeping a bad house" was just another example of phrases used to describe a whorehouse nicely. Unlike Frances's, Sarah's arrest appeared in the local newspaper and not in the jail register.

Sarah did not learn her lesson. She was rearrested in late May. Once again, she was charged with keeping a bad house. Her husband, Louis, was arrested at the same time for selling liquor on Sunday and keeping a saloon open on Sunday.

Less than two months later, Louis Halliday died. According to his obituary, he had been sick for two weeks, but his death was unexpected.

By 1902, Sarah had turned her life around. She was boarding at 133 North Third Street in Ironton.

Just eight years later, the federal census recorded Sarah as a boardinghouse owner. Her boardinghouse was located on North Third Street in Ironton. She had two boarders, George Bush and Blanch Ferguson. Although Sarah had given birth to three children, none of them were still living in 1910. She was only thirty-nine years old.

Sarah's story ends there. She disappears from the city directories and other records.

Male Prostitutes

Not all prostitutes were women. Men, too, found themselves working in the oldest profession. Thomas Morahan was arrested on April 13, 1882, for prostitution. He was released the following day. If he faced any other punishment for his crimes, it was not recorded in the jail register. Thomas did have another job. He worked as a nail feeder at Ironton's Belfont Iron Works. His home was on the corner on Sixth and Etna. The 1882 arrest was the only time Thomas was arrested in Lawrence County, Ohio.

DELCIE HOSKINS

Both Frances and Sarah were listed as white women, but Ironton had women of color who operated whorehouses. One notable example was Delcie Hoskins. Hoskins was described as having a dark complexion. Her house of ill fame was located on the corner of Eighth Street and Adams in Ironton.

In November 1915, Captain Barney Smith, Officer Justus, Officer Mckee and Officer Howard raided her house. The police had to make three trips to transfer all the people they had arrested. Among those arrested were four young women of color. Sixteen men were also arrested that day. Most of the men arrested worked for contractor Simpson on the new Portsmouth traction line.

Delcie had been warned the previous week to leave town. She ignored the warning.

Unlike most of the people arrested for prostitution, Delcie would serve more than a month. Most prostitutes paid a fine and served a few days in jail. Perhaps the local law wanted to teach her a lesson.

MARY B. NEFF

Not all convicted of prostitution were adults. Nor did they begin with such a serious crime. Mary B. Neff was born on July 20, 1881. She was the daughter of Robert and Amanda J. Neff. Her father worked for the railroad as a laborer. Her childhood seemed typical and safe. It certainly did not appear to lead one to believe she was a troubled child. Appearances, however, can be deceiving.

Mary was arrested for the first time on April 14, 1895. The crime was listed as "incorrigible." She was in the local jail for six days before being transferred to the Ohio Girls' Industrial School. Her father and the local courts both were responsible for sending her to the industrial school.

The Girls' Industrial School was formed in 1869 by the Ohio General Assembly. The school's purpose was to take in "exposed, helpless, evil disposed and vicious girls." Located north of Columbus, Ohio, the 109 acres had once been the location of the White Sulfur Springs health resort. Girls from the age of eight to twenty-one were incarcerated for willfulness and disobedience.

On April 20, 1895, Mary was admitted to the industrial school. According to the school records, Mary had little education but could read and write. She was sent to the school for her incorrigible behavior. What that behavior may have consisted of was not recorded. She remained at the school for four years.

On July 7, 1899, Mary was able to leave the industrial school. She was not able to return to her parents in Lawrence County. She was instead indentured to Mr. O.D. Maizis and his family. The Maizises lived in Columbus, Ohio. The school would receive reports from the family about Mary and her conduct. Sadly for Mary, the reports received were rarely good.

By December 1900, Mary had returned to Lawrence County. On December 14, 1900, she was arrested once again for incorrigible behavior. The jail registry claims she returned to the industrial school after spending four days in the local jail; however, she does not appear in the industrial school records again.

Mary's troubles were far from over. Her incarceration in the industrial school seemed to have little effect. In February 1901, she was arrested for cutting. Mary's cutting would lead her to be incarcerated in the local jail until April 9, 1901.

Just two months after her release, Mary was once again arrested. This time she was charged with prostitution on June 24, 1901. She was released on August 31, 1901.

Her story ends there. Hopefully, her tale ended happily. However, her life up to that point had been far from happy. One wonders what would have happened if she had received treatment instead of punishment.

Pansy Williams and Nora Gambel

In May 1907, two women made the local newspaper for crimes associated with whorehouses.

Nora Gambel's home on North Third Street in Ironton was raided by the local police. The police found fourteen girls from nearby cities residing there. It was not unheard of for people to bring girls from Kentucky and West Virginia to work in the Ironton houses in the red-light district. Gambel was charged with harboring an underage girl.

Pansy Williams appeared in the same newspaper as Gambel. A warrant had been issued for Pansy's arrest. A fifteen-year-old girl had gone missing in West Virginia. She was located in Pansy Williams's house by Chief Brice of Ironton. The charge was not listed, but one assumes she was charged with harboring or prostituting a minor. Williams was taken before Chief Ross on May 5, 1907. The results were not recorded.

Streetwalkers

Some women and men did not work in an actual house of ill fame. Some worked on the street. Their arrest records listed their crime as streetwalking. Among those who were charged with this crime was Sarah E. Kingery, arrested on October 13, 1890. She would spend four days in jail.

James Stutler was arrested for streetwalking just a week after Thomas. He served one day in jail before being released.

Enticing Children

In some cases, women keeping houses of ill repute would search for new employees. If they were caught, they would face the charge of enticing a girl or child. Two women in Lawrence County faced such charges. They faced drastically different punishments.

Matilda Beatty, aged sixty-five, was arrested on March 9, 1905, for "enticing child." She remained in the local jail for nearly a month. On April 6, 1905, Matilda was transferred to the Ohio State Penitentiary.

Jennie Duskins was charged with "enticing girl" three years later. She served only one day in the local jail before being released.

Other Crimes

Prostitution was not the only activity going on in the red-light district. Numerous other crimes flourished in the rough areas surrounding the houses of ill fame.

In June 1885, a man named Lawrence Sloan chose to visit a local whorehouse and lost his life. Sloan had decided to pretend to be a police officer when he entered the establishment. Within the business, he found Michael Carr. For an unknown reason, Sloan attempted to arrest Carr. Carr chose not to go quietly. He grabbed a club and struck Sloan. Sloan fell to the floor with a broken jaw and possibly a cracked skull. Sloan passed away from his injuries. Carr was arrested and held on a $500 bond.

In January 1878, four or five people were involved in a shooting at a pike north of Ironton. The police did not know exactly how many were involved. One man was shot through his arm. He was supposedly not hurt badly even though he was shot. Warrants had been issued for everyone else involved.

THE FBI RAID OF 1947

No one can discuss prostitution in Lawrence County, Ohio, without mentioning the FBI raid of 1947. Ironton's reputation for corruption and crime caught the federal government's attention. In fact, the city had become the focal point of prostitution for the industrial towns in Ohio, Kentucky and West Virginia. The red-light district had been operating for sixty years. It was known locally as the Line.

At the time, the local police and sheriff's departments were believed to be so corrupt that the federal agents could not even involve them in their investigation. Fifty FBI agents met in nearby Scioto County, Ohio, to plan their raid.

The FBI director, J. Edgar Hoover, had announced the raid.

The raid could be considered a success: a total of forty-nine people were arrested. The initial raid resulted in the arrest of twenty-eight women and fifteen men. Among those arrested were Arthur Hall, James Williams Mills, Ollie Nichols, Elby Paul Brown, Jean Elizabeth Foster, Marjorie Gibson and Emma Nichols.

The remaining arrests would occur as far away as California. One man and one woman were arrested in Columbus, Ohio. Another two people were caught in Benld, Illinois. One woman was arrested in St. Louis, Missouri, and another in San Francisco, California.

Eleven people were charged with interstate transportation of girls for purposes of prostitution. If found guilty, they would face a $5,000 fine, five years in prison or both.

In the whorehouses, the agents recovered a variety of weapons: pistols, shotguns and hundreds of rounds of ammunition. Some daggers were

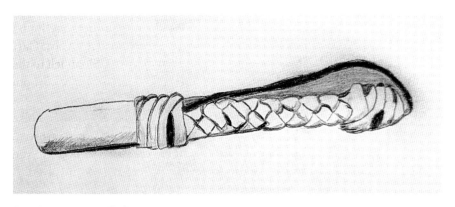

Blackjack. *Author's collection.*

among the weapons as well. Lastly, they found blackjacks. Blackjacks are leather pouches filled with some form of metal. Easily concealed in pockets, they were handy tools in the illegal trade.

2

CONTINENTAL NITE CLUB

The Continental Nite Club went by many names. Continental Club. Club Continental. All refer to a nightclub located in Chesapeake, Ohio, in the 1940s. The club would become a major attraction for visitors to the tristate area and a source of controversy in Ohio.

The club was officially owned by the Chesapeake Operating Company. The president of the club was Jack Goodman. A.E. Giessy was the club's vice president, while E.W. Sauers was the secretary.

For most of us, those names do not sound familiar, but the people they are associated with are another story. All three men had ties to the Cleveland Syndicate.

The Cleveland Syndicate was an organized crime enterprise operating out of Cleveland, Ohio. The syndicate was formed in the 1920s by Morris Kleinman, Louis Rothkopf, Sam Tucker and Moe Davis. When Prohibition took over the nation, these men organized a fleet of boats on Lake Erie. These boats, known as the Big Jewish Navy, brought liquor from Canada to Cleveland. Rumrunning and other illegal enterprises made the syndicate one of the wealthiest organizations in Cleveland's mobs.

With their profits from bootlegging, the Cleveland Syndicate invested in gambling casinos. Its members became such a threat that they were forced out of Cleveland in 1935 by the reform mayor Harold Burton.

When they could no longer operate their illegal businesses in Cleveland, the men moved them to other locations in Ohio. They chose places where officials could be paid to ignore their activities. One of the places they chose was Chesapeake, Ohio.

Continental Nite Club. *Author's collection.*

MOE DAVIS

Moe Davis was the most powerful of the syndicate members. Also known as Moe Dalitz, he was the boss of the notorious Mayfield Road Gang. He was a known associate of Lucky Luciano and the absolute boss of Cleveland's underworld in the 1930s. Originally from Detroit, Davis first lived in Akron, Ohio, before moving to Cleveland. He was so connected to the major mob bosses in the United States that if anyone questioned his authority, they would find themselves answering to Lucky Luciano, Meyer Lansky and Bugsy Siegel.

Davis's business was not limited to Ohio. He owned 66 percent of the Stardust Hotel in Las Vegas, Nevada. He paid over $66,000 to assist in the merger between Detroit Steel Company and Reliance Steel of Cleveland in 1945. His assistance in the merger brought him $230,000 in profits. He also ran resort hotels in Florida.

Davis's activities would result in him testifying before the U.S. Senate. During his testimony, he was labeled an ex-bootlegger and a gambling figure.

LOUIS ROTHKOPF

Known as Uncle Louis, Louis Rothkopf was a native of Cleveland. He was known for traveling to meet other businessmen who liked to bend the laws like him. One of his friends was Frank Costello, a New York racketeer. Louis made his mark in Cleveland's underground by overseeing the construction of illegal distilleries in Cleveland during the 1920s.

MORRIS KLEINMAN

Like Louis Rothkopf, Morris Kleinman was a native of Cleveland, Ohio. He had taken over his father's lucrative poultry business at an early age but found himself becoming bored with such honest work. He became a boxer and even won Cleveland's lightweight championship. Morris would later dabble in bookmaking and brewery operations before joining the Cleveland Syndicate. Unlike the other members of the syndicate, Morris had been convicted for tax evasion and spent three years in prison.

CONTINENTAL CLUB

When they were kicked out of Cleveland, the syndicate relocated to other cities in Ohio. They used their subordinates to run these facilities for them.

The Continental Club's day-to-day operations were under the supervision of William and Howard Schwartz.

It did not take long for the club to become a destination for anyone looking for a good time in the tristate. Important visitors to Huntington and Charleston, West Virginia, would gladly cross the Ohio for a good time gambling and drinking at the Continental.

The Explosion

With the club's popularity on the rise, trouble was not far behind. On September 27, 1939, the club's compressor exploded. Pressure had built up within the compressor's tank, causing the explosion. The metal of the tank was blown through the floor, and it damaged the building's air-conditioning unit. A newspaper article claimed no one was injured in the incident, but that proved to be false.

In September 1941, George Paulos sued the club, claiming he had been injured when the compressor blew up. According to Paulos, he had spent significant time in the Guthrie Hospital in Huntington, West Virginia, and Mountain State Hospital in Charleston, West Virginia, recovering from his injuries. For his pain and suffering, he sought $2,999.

Liquor License Troubles

In 1945, the Continental's liquor license was in danger of being revoked. Liquor director Robert M. Sohngen was questioning whether they could have liquor and gambling in the same location. To fix the issue, the owners just built a casino next to the main club. Thus they were able to keep their license and keep their gambling business.

Robbery

In late April 1948, the club was the location of a robbery. Around 2:30 p.m., men with submachine guns or tommy guns entered the club and held up the forty patrons and employees inside. Some victims said there were four men, while others said seven. Some witnesses claimed the leader appeared to have been a man in his mid-fifties.

The men lined the patrons up against a wall and deprived them of their valuables one by one. One employee attempted to save a diamond ring by hiding it in his mouth, but the thieves were not fooled. The ring joined the rest of the loot. The men also took several car keys from their victims.

Tommy gun. *Author's collection.*

Although the thieves ignored the slot machines, they were determined to have the contents of the safe. In fact, they waited a long time for the safe to be opened. Oddly, they did not seem overly concerned about the length of time needed to get the safe open.

The men were in the club for approximately an hour. It was later estimated that they had netted $100,000 in cash and other valuables.

Before they left, the men took time to get a drink from the bar. Patrons heard the sound of three cars starting and driving away.

No one made any attempt to see where the thieves were heading. Some suggested it sounded like they were heading toward Cincinnati, but no one knew for sure.

Judge James H. Collier. *Briggs Lawrence County Public Library, Hamner Room.*

What really made this robbery unique is that no one wanted to report it. Only a salesman who had lost his wallet and keys to his car in the robbery reported the theft. He seemed to think the robbing of the patrons was more of an afterthought.

The staff and other victims were reluctant to discuss the robbery. In fact, the first reporting of the robbery occurred fourteen hours after the men had left the club.

The common pleas judge James H. Collier had questions about the whole incident. He feared something much worse was going on at the club. Collier believed the club was getting permission to operate in violation of the law.

Governor Frank J. Lausche

The judge was not the only one who had grown suspicious of the Continental Club. Governor Frank J. Lausche began a crusade against the various gambling dens of the Cleveland Syndicate. Lawrence County was on his radar.

In August 1945, the governor stated that gambling was running rampant in Lawrence County, Ohio. He demanded Sheriff Milton B. Rucker and Mayor R.L. Hamilton start cleaning up Chesapeake. If they would not or could not, the governor had no problem doing the job for them.

To prove his point, Governor Lausche had evidence. He had obtained photographs showing gambling taking place fifty feet from the club, with

Governor Frank J. Lausche.
Author's collection.

the club managers' and owners' participation. He also stated the club's casino had twenty slot machines, dice tables, poker tables and horse race betting.

With so much evidence facing them, Mayor Hamilton and Sheriff Rucker agreed to help clean up Chesapeake.

The governor did not just target Chesapeake. His sights were set on the Pettibone Club in Bainbridge Township, Geauga County, Ohio; Jungle Inn in Liberty Township, Warren County, Ohio; and Mounds Club in Lake County, Ohio.

The Pettibone Club was one of the first clubs to face the governor's ire. Lausche declared he would shut down the club in a press conference on May 22, 1946. Describing the club as a gambling den, he ordered a grand jury investigation. Lausche vowed he would do anything he could legally do to close the club.

More Lawsuits

In June 1948, Reuben Gordon from Hazard, Kentucky, filed a civil suit against the Continental Club as well as William and Howard Schwartz. He alleged he had been injured when he was thrown out of the club on July 2, 1945. Gordon was asking for over $41,000 for his damages. Unfortunately for him, Judge Druffel dismissed the case.

In January 1948, F.A. Copenhaven filed a suit against the club to recoup money he had lost there. A resident of Huntington, West Virginia, Copenhaven claimed he had lost $5,100 while gambling at the club from December 12, 1948, to December 19, 1948. Like Gorden, he was unsuccessful.

Raids on Local Illegal Activities

On February 25, 1949, the Lawrence County sheriff and other officials launched their first attempt to clean up their county. A series of massive raids were conducted on five local pool halls. The raids resulted in fifty people being arrested. Of that number, forty-two pleaded guilty. Four cases were dismissed.

Oddly, the Continental Club was not mentioned in the raids.

The Governor Continues to Clean Up Ohio

In 1949, Governor Lausche's crusade gained momentum. He was able to get the Continental Club's liquor license revoked, which drastically affected the business.

In March 1949, the Continental Club was under surveillance. The owners tried to limit what could be seen or reported to the authorities. They began demanding visitors must be members of the club. If they were not members, they must have a proper recommendation from a member. People entering the club were secretly watched through peepholes without their knowledge. The owners and managers also used mirrors to help observe their customers without their knowledge.

Inside, members and their guests could still find the luxury they had enjoyed in the past. Overstuffed chairs and divans were scattered throughout the club. Valets and maids were stationed in the men's and women's lounges to attend to the needs of the patrons. In the ladies' lounges, women would find free cosmetics so they could further beautify themselves.

As for gambling, the club boasted a variety of options. The twenty slot machines had increased to forty-five. Gamblers could keep track of their bets by observing the club's racing returns. Tables were set up for blackjack, dice, poker and roulette games. The Continental even had a chuck-a-luck, where patrons gambled on three dice. They would win if they guessed the numbers that would appear on the roll of the dice.

Governor Lausche denounced the multimillion-dollar gambling operations. He proposed two laws should be passed to aid his efforts. A special hearing was held on March 15, 1949, to hear his proposals.

The first law would allow the governor to remove any sheriff from office if that person was not performing his duties. Of course, the governor was the one who would evaluate what constituted good performance.

Sheriff Stewart Harlan of Geauga County, Ohio, strongly objected to the senate bill. He felt he did not need the governor or the state to tell him how to do his job. In his opinion, if he was not performing well, the voters would let him know. All they had to do was vote him out of office.

The second proposed law gave more power to the county prosecutors and Ohio state attorney general. The law, if passed, would allow those officeholders to padlock any gambling establishments within their jurisdiction.

Since Governor Lausche could not introduce the bills himself, Senator William H. Daugherty, a Democrat from Columbiana County, Ohio, would do so on his behalf. Interestingly, there were no businesses being targeted by the governor in Columbiana County.

The governor was at least partially successful. The Mounds Club near Willoughby in Lake County, Ohio, did close. However, the closure was only for a few months.

Judge James Collier

The governor was not the only one taking a hard stance against the gambling dens. Lawrence County common pleas judge James Collier was ready to eliminate gambling businesses in his county.

He had become suspicious of the Continental Club after the robbery in April 1948. He ordered a special grand jury to be impaneled to investigate the Continental. Working with Prosecutor Louis Sheridan, he wanted to get the men behind the scenes. He knew these men were bribing local politicians and residents to keep quiet. Money was being paid to someone to protect the club, and he wanted to know who was paying and who was being paid.

The Continental Club Closes

In October 1949, the Continental Club closed its doors. The club had been denied its D-5 nightclub permit by the permit chief, Francis K. Cole. Cole was part of the Ohio State Department of Liquor Control. He had finally been able to revoke the Continental's liquor license.

When Cole traveled to Lawrence County to inspect the club, he was surprised to find the club closed. Upon closer inspection, he discovered the place looked completely abandoned, as if it had been closed for some time.

The Continental Club was not alone. Once the governor realized the four clubs he had targeted appeared to be owned by the same people, his battle became progressively stronger. In the end, his efforts caused the closure of the Mounds Club and Jungle Inn as well.

In December 1949, the state liquor department raided the Continental Club. Led by state liquor enforcement chief A.A. Rutkowski, the authorities confiscated forty slot machines.

The Continental Club did try to reopen. The owners went to the Ohio Supreme Court, requesting Judge Collier be removed from their case. Their request was denied.

A New Beginning

In December 1960, Stanley Evans, president of Evans Grocery Company, announced his company was going to be building a small shopping center on the former Continental Club site. The development would cost over $1 million when completed. Construction was to begin in the spring of 1961. The new center would open that summer.

3

SISTER-IN-LAW FROM HELL

*J*ust as the American Civil War was tearing our country apart, a family at Mount Vernon Furnace was facing its own destruction. On April 23, 1863, Nancy Johnson was pronounced dead at the tender age of twenty. Neighbors had described Nancy as a peaceful, quiet and "inoffensive woman." Those who knew Nancy saw a vibrant, healthy young woman. Neighbors, friends and family were shocked to hear of her death.

The daughter of Andrew and Susan Dempsey, Nancy had been recently married. On August 17, 1861, Nancy was united in marriage to Robert Johnson in Lawrence County, Ohio. After their marriage, the couple settled near the Mount Vernon Furnace.

Not everyone was as happy about the Johnsons' marriage. Robert's sister, Rachel Rose, was not enamored of her new sister-in-law. On more than one occasion, Rachel threatened Nancy. Community members hurling insults at Nancy was not an uncommon occurrence. During a local party, Rachel threatened to strike Nancy with a dipper of water.

Robert often felt put in the middle of his sister and wife. In a conversation with a neighbor, David Lodge, Robert complained of the constant quarreling between the two women. He realized his sister, Rachel, was the source of the problems. He wished Rachel would just stop. He would get his wish, but not in the manner he was expecting.

When Robert announced his wife's sudden death, an inquest was immediately completed. Esquire Hanley was summoned to lead the examination.

Mount Vernon Furnace. *Author's collection.*

Only four people were in the house when Nancy's untimely death occurred. Nancy was unable to testify. Robert and Nancy's baby, Sarah, had been lying in the cradle near the bed where her mother died but was too young to relate what she witnessed. That left only Robert and Rachel.

The siblings were quick to tell their sad tale. They said Nancy had been standing by her pie safe when she suddenly began to have a "fit." By fit, they meant Nancy had experienced some form of seizure. The seizure caused Nancy to fall and further injure herself.

Robert carried his ailing wife to their bedroom. He laid her out on their marriage bed to watch her die before help could be summoned.

That evening, Esquire Hanley was brought in for an inquest. Friends and family alike wanted answers. Nancy's father, Andrew Dempsey, was especially suspicious about his daughter's death. He had sent for the doctor in the first place. When Hanley was finished, his verdict of natural death was not what Nancy's family wanted to hear. In fact, they demanded more doctors examine her body. They demanded another inquest into her death.

Dr. Moxley and Dr. Cory were the second and third doctors to examine poor Nancy's body. These doctors found evidence that directly countered the statements of Robert and Rachel.

Nancy's once healthy, vibrant body was now battered and broken. The body was covered with minor bruises that could be evidence of a fall, but there were also more serious injuries. Those injuries could not be easily explained. Her spine had been fractured between the shoulders. The back of the skull had also been fractured. Lastly, her neck was dislocated. These injuries proved something more than a fall had taken place.

Esquire Warneke was brought in for the second inquest. J.S. Roadarmour was appointed to act as a special constable. Fifteen witnesses were called in to testify at the second trial.

Many people took the stand to tell of hostilities between Rachel and Nancy. Witnesses testified that Rachel was often heard threatening and insulting her sister-in-law. One person recalled Rachel threatening Nancy over a dipper of water while the two women were at a local party.

Another person witnessed threats just before Nancy's "accident." Nancy had made some comments that made their way back to Rachel. What those comments may have been was not mentioned. However, they were enough to prompt Rachel to threaten to whip Nancy just a few days before Nancy's death.

David Lodge was one witness to testify to the long, continual feud between Rachel and Nancy. David had heard Rachel threaten to whip Nancy to death. He also spoke to Robert, Nancy's husband and Rachel's brother, about the constant fighting between the two women. It was his belief that Rachel was the aggressor in most if not all the confrontations. Robert just wanted it all to stop. Caught in the middle, Robert was the one who was forced to witness the regular attacks by Rachel on his wife.

Just before Nancy was killed, Isaac Wollem, a neighbor, saw Rachel approaching the Johnson house. Rachel's appearance prompted him to ask what was wrong. Wollem said Rachel was "very mad." Her sleeves were rolled up as if she was prepared to begin a difficult job. Rachel's replies to his inquiries gave further evidence of her ever-rising anger.

Six men were seated as the jury. A. Trapp, John McCall, John Spear, R.J. Marshall and Hugh Livingston were chosen to hear the case. Robert Scott was chosen as the foreman.

After all the testimony had been heard and evidence examined, the jury members were ready to share their verdict: "Death caused by a blow from some heavy, hard substance, probably a club, in the hands of Rachel Rose inflicted with intent to kill."

On February 23, 1864, Rachel Rose was sentenced to ten years for manslaughter. Apparently, the jury did not believe Rachel had planned the murder. The manslaughter ruling means her anger may have caused her to kill her sister-in-law. Perhaps their long, drawn-out disagreements were destined to end in tragedy.

Ohio State Penitentiary. *Author's collection.*

Robert Johnson did not escape lady justice. On the same day as his sister was sentenced, Robert was sentenced to seven years at the Ohio State Penitentiary. He, too, was convicted of manslaughter.

In May 1869, the *Ironton Register*, one of the older newspapers in Ironton, published a list of Lawrence County residents at the Ohio State Penitentiary. Both Rachel Rose and Robert Johnson were still serving their time behind bars.

At the penitentiary, prisoners, if well-behaved, were given jobs. Most of these would support the jail and supply much-needed food and other products. Rachel had been placed in a position where she sewed and washed the clothes of other inmates. Robert worked in the agricultural section. Both were reported to have good conduct while incarcerated.

Sarah Johnson, Robert and Nancy's daughter, was placed in the custody of her maternal grandparents. In the 1880 Federal Census, she is listed as living with Andrew Dempsey and his second wife, Melissa.

As for Robert Johnson and Rachel Rose, they disappear from history. They did not return to Lawrence County, Ohio, after their release. They made a new life for themselves elsewhere.

4

CRIMES OF THE INNOCENT

*O*ften in small communities, people have drastically different viewpoints on certain subjects and people. Judge Lloyd Burwell would be an example for Lawrence Countians.

If you grew up in Lawrence County during the 1980s and 1990s, you were warned about appearing before Judge Burwell. He was known to be extremely tough on juveniles who entered his courtroom. Such strictness brought about less crime, but many would say it went too far.

In the end, the judge would capture the interest of the nation and inspire a TV movie starring Andy Griffith.

Lloyd Burwell was born on June 20, 1925, in Rock Creek, Lawrence County, Ohio. He was the son of Orlo and Maide Warren Burwell. Although he started his life in Lawrence County, his family moved to Oklahoma before he could graduate from high school. Central High School in Oklahoma City, Oklahoma, would be his alma mater.

After high school, Burwell returned to Ohio. He studied at Ohio University and graduated from there in 1950. Then, he received his law degree from Ohio Northern University's College of Law in 1953.

He immediately began practicing law.

In December 1959, Burwell sought to be nominated in the May 1960 primary on the Republican ticket as the Lawrence County prosecutor. At the age of thirty-four, he had been practicing law for only six years. However, he succeeded in becoming the Republican nominee. Sadly, he lost that November to the Democratic nominee, Dennis Callahan. This election would be his first dip into politics. It would be far from his last.

Central High School, Oklahoma City, Oklahoma. *Author's collection.*

Burwell remained active within the community. He played a major role in the local Boy Scout troops. In 1970, he became the Scioto Area Boy Scout Council president.

Burwell continued to seek other ways to serve his community. He was elected as the Chesapeake solicitor. Later, he served as the Ironton municipal judge for two years.

In 1976, Governor James Rhodes appointed Judge Burwell to the Lawrence County Court of Common Pleas. It was in this position that his no-nonsense stands gained attention.

During the spring of 1977, Judge Burwell submitted a purchase order for supplies and equipment for the juvenile and probate court totaling $1,000. The county commissioners refused to pay the invoice. They claimed the judge had not followed proper procedure in requesting the purchases. It seems the judge had jumped the gun a bit. He had ordered the supplies before he had actually taken the office on January 2, 1988.

Burwell informed the commissioners, "I don't have to follow your procedures." Following his own convictions, Judge Burwell had two county commissioners jailed. President W.H. Kaiser and Commissioner Mark Malone were the two men who found themselves behind bars. Their time in jail was short-lived. The Fourth Court of Appeals, located in Steubenville, ruled the two men be released after only two hours.

Adults were not the only group to face Burwell's wrath. He firmly believed that society had been coddling kids for over twenty years, and he was going to be making changes.

In January 1978, Judge Burwell instituted a new rule for truancy. For every day skipped from school, a juvenile would spend one day in jail. They would not be forced to join the general population of juvenile offenders but would be kept separate. This new rule was strictly enforced. The truancy numbers dropped countywide from 25 percent to only 5 percent.

Juvenile crime also saw a dramatic drop under Burwell's first few years. All crimes committed by juveniles dropped by 22 percent.

The community was happy to see kids back in school and the crime rates drop. Still, some questioned the severity of some of his punishments.

In November 1979, Judge Burwell gained attention for a ruling that was considered unnecessarily harsh and possibly illegal. A Lawrence County couple had been caught neglecting and abusing their adopted son. Joe Ed and Eva Moore stood accused of locking their son in a cage each night, failing to feed him or even provide a sanitary environment for him to live in. As a result, their four-year-old son was malnourished and emotionally disturbed.

Once his living arrangements were known, the boy was immediately removed from the Moore home. He was placed in the care of the state, where he would receive the care he so desperately needed.

Lawrence County, Ohio Court House. *Briggs Lawrence County Public Library, Hamner Room.*

One would think the Moores could not defend themselves, but they had excuses for their actions. They had placed the boy in a cage to keep him from falling out of bed. As for not feeding him, they fed him when he asked for food. If he did not ask for food, he was not given food. For them, it was simple.

Thankfully, no one else saw it that way. The couple was convicted and taken before Burwell for sentencing.

Judge Burwell, disgusted by the horrible treatment of the boy, ordered the Moores to jail. Joe Ed was to serve nine days, and his wife was to serve seven days. But the judge was not finished. He also ordered the Moores to be given only bread and water during their incarceration. The county prosecutor, Randy Lambert, advised the judge that his sentence was illegal. In the end, the couple had no such restriction implemented. Burwell's original decision did attract notice from across the state—and not the type Lawrence County wanted.

As for the Moores, they served their time in jail without any further punishment. Joe Ed was even allowed to leave the jail daily to go to ARMCO to work. Moore had four children to support, not including the one removed from his care.

Although Judge Burwell was horrified by the sad treatment of the four-year-old, juveniles appearing in his courtroom did not find a sympathetic ear. In 1979 alone, Judge Burwell incarcerated 178 juveniles in Lawrence County. They served an average of five days. While in jail, they were forced to wear institutional-style coveralls. They were not supplied with toothpaste, toothbrushes, soap or shampoo. Such supplies could only be purchased from the jail's commissary by family members.

Once in the jail, the juveniles would not be permitted to leave the cell block unless seeing visitors. Phone calls were prohibited regardless of whether they were to their parents, ministers or friends. The only time they could receive visitors was on Tuesdays and Thursdays. If they had someone to see them, they could talk only while standing in the jail hallway.

Judge Burwell used other methods to punish kids who appeared before him. First, children could find themselves charged with crimes that were not even illegal for adults. For instance, juveniles could be sentenced to jail for not going to school or staying out past curfew.

Before the children even entered the county jail, the judge began to punish parents and juveniles. He would deliberately delay detention hearings, resulting in juveniles being incarcerated for longer than necessary. Thus he separated the parents from their children before the cases even began.

Lawrence County, Ohio Jail. *Briggs Lawrence County Public Library, Hamner Room.*

In his courtroom, the judge used his power to intimidate parents and children alike. A large paddle was kept in the courtroom for parents to use on their children as punishment. The decision to use corporal punishment was made by the judge, not the parents. Burwell believed part of the problem was the lack of discipline the children received at home. He chose to correct this lack within the courtroom.

In pursuing justice, Judge Burwell often bent or completely broke the law. He allowed information illegally obtained to be used in court. He harassed, intimidated and threatened defendants into waiving their constitutional rights. Innocent and guilty could find themselves facing arrest without probable cause.

Once convicted, defendants might face a variety of punishments. Judge Burwell threatened more than one person with jail time if they did not leave the county. Some people faced corporal punishment. Others were jailed.

Judge Burwell slowly became a boogeyman to children all over the tristate. Children were warned by their parents: if they did not behave, they would face Burwell. Unlike the fictional boogeyman, Burwell was all too real.

In June 1980, Burwell made the news again for disagreements involving the county commissioners. The courthouse and other Lawrence County offices were starting to preserve their records by microfilming them. By microfilming the records, they could free up space within the courthouse. Judge Burwell issued orders from his bench requiring the county commissioners and the clerk of court, Dale Burcham, to expedite the microfilming of the juvenile court records.

Burwell felt the process was taking too long. Court records were being kept in the unsecure hallways of the courthouse until they could be filmed. The commissioners pointed out that the juvenile court had a special room set aside to house the records. If the judge used the room, he should have plenty of room to house his records in a secure location until filming. Burwell disagreed. The room in question had been repurposed to become a private lunchroom for the juvenile court. The judge stated he needed the private lunchroom because he spent so much time working through lunch. The judge went on to demand another room to be cleared out to make room for his records.

The judge did offer another solution. He offered to send $2,000 from the juvenile court fund to speed up the transcription and filming process. Those funds were set aside to pay for attorney fees to be given to lawyers appointed by the court to represent defendants—not to pay for transcriptions and record preservation.

Included in the judicial order concerning the record preservation was another seemingly unrelated item. Judge Burwell had demanded two new attorney tables be purchased for his courtroom. His request had been denied because the court's current tables were unmarred. The commissioners saw no reason to purchase new ones. Once the judge issued an order to the commissioners and clerk of court from his bench, they gave in.

With his unorthodox behavior and sentencing, it is not shocking that Judge Lloyd Burwell crossed the line. He found himself facing a judge. Two juveniles sued Burwell in civil court for the mistreatment and abuse they suffered as a result of the judge's decisions.

Since they were juveniles, the two kids would only be known under the aliases Deborah Doe and Robert Roe. Deborah Doe filed first and faced Judge Burwell first. Deborah was a fifteen-year-old girl. She had been a good kid, but a late-night trip with a friend landed her before the judge. Under normal circumstances, she would not have even faced jail time, but things were not normal in Lawrence County. First, she was charged with running away from home. Although the charges were false, Deborah was taken into custody in February 1981. She appeared before the judge and was sentenced to the Lawrence County jail.

Sadly, Deborah's story gets worse, not better. While in the jail, she was exposed to unlawful practices and conditions, according to her court filing.

Specifically, Deborah was sexually assaulted by a deputy jailer and two adult inmates.

Once released from jail, Deborah was placed on probation until the end of 1981. Since she was a juvenile, much of her case is sealed. If her assault affected her sentence or probation, it was not recorded.

Just a few months after Deborah was arrested, another Lawrence County youth found himself before the judge. Known as Robert Roe, the sixteen-year-old was charged with theft. He appeared before the judge in April 1981.

In August 1981, House Bill 440 gave Judge Burwell even more power. The state house of representatives decided juveniles would serve their jail terms locally rather than be transferred to juvenile facilities in other parts of Ohio.

Deborah Doe and Robert Roe filed their own lawsuit. Deborah's father, alias John Doe, and Robert's father, Richard Roe, were listed as co-plaintiffs. They sued Judge Lloyd Burwell, Mark A. Malone, Donald Lambert, Carl T. Baker, Lawrence County sheriff Daniel Hieronimus and Lawrence County, Ohio. The plaintiffs accused the judge of violating their First, Fourth, Fifth, Ninth and Fourteenth Amendment constitutional rights.

Doe and Roe won their case. They received relatively small amounts compared to lawsuits today. Robert Roe received $3,500. Deborah received $37,000.

Although their true identities were protected during the court proceedings, they probably did not remain anonymous. In a small town like Ironton, secrets are hard to keep. Everyone knows everyone. Such a sensational story would not be easy to keep under wraps.

The lawsuit brought about two major events. First, Judge Burwell agreed to stop incarcerating juveniles after April 1982. The judge, however, admitted to no wrongdoing.

The second event was to bring national attention to Ironton, Ohio. Deborah and Robert's cases were used as the basis for a made-for-TV movie. Before crime TV, the ID channel or *COPS*, made-for-TV movies brought true crime into our homes. Inspired by reality, these movies were often must-see television.

In 1985, *Crime of Innocence* aired. Andy Griffith played the Judge Lloyd Burwell character, named Judge Julius Sullivan. Known for his lovable characters, Griffith strayed into new territory for this role. The movie centers on the story of a family trying to find justice for their daughter, who was sexually assaulted when unjustly incarcerated. When she cannot find help with the local law enforcement, her family has to seek justice elsewhere.

Nearly every household in the tristate would have tuned in to watch the story in 1985. The library still receives requests to add the movie to their collection. The movie has not appeared on DVD or BluRay. A grainy version can be located on YouTube, if you know where to look.

Judge Lloyd Burwell served eight years as a juvenile court judge as well as a probate court judge and Ironton Municipal Court judge. When he died in 1995 at the age of seventy, his colleagues mentioned the many new ideas he brought to the probate court, some of which still appear today. They talked about how he was well respected among his peers. Lastly, they mentioned his "colorful courtroom personality."

The community remains split. Some recognize the many improvements Burwell brought to Lawrence County, while others cannot forget or forgive the harm he caused.

5

CHARLES SHAFER

Husband, Father, Murderer

Charles Wesley Shafer was born in Lawrence County, Ohio, on February 16, 1872. He was the son of Coonrod and Tacy Elizabeth Shafer.

Coonrod was a Civil War veteran and descendant of German immigrants. He had married Tacy on March 7, 1861, just before going off to fight in the war.

After the war, Coonrod and Tacy had made their family home in Union Township, Lawrence County, Ohio. He supported his growing family by farming. In memory of his time as a soldier and to honor the man who brought an end to the war, he named his son Ulysses Grant.

Tacy would deliver four children during her union with Coonrod. Ulysses Grant was born in 1867. Simon Peter followed his older brother just a year later. The Shafers welcomed their first and only daughter, Barbara Ellen, in 1870. Charles Wesley was their final son and child.

For all appearances, Charles had a normal childhood. He did lose his father after he reached adulthood, but he appeared to have already begun his own life. He still resided with his mother, as most young unmarried men did.

One of his first jobs would be in Wilgus, Lawrence County, Ohio. He was appointed postmaster of Wilgus on December 19, 1896. Wilgus was just one of several small villages located in Mason Township, Lawrence County, Ohio. In 1890, the township boasted a little over 1,700 residents. Although he was the local postmaster, Charles continued to work on the family farm where he lived with his mother.

On February 20, 1905, Charles Wesley Shafer married Carrie Brammer. Born just five years after her new husband in Windsor Township, Lawrence County, Ohio, Carrie was the daughter of John and Susan Payne Brammer.

Charles was not Carrie's first husband. In fact, she had been married to another man, named Shaffer. No record of her first marriage could be found. One would assume her husband had passed away prior to 1900 but after early 1898.

The evidence of the marriage can be inferred by the one child born from the union. Hershel Lester Shaffer was born on September 7, 1898, in Union Township, Lawrence County, Ohio.

In 1900, Carrie and Hershel were living with her brother Ellis Brammer and her sister Sarah in Union Township, Lawrence County, Ohio.

Carrie had found employment as a local schoolteacher. She became quite popular and was well respected by her students and their parents. Such an honored position would not have been opened to anyone with less than an honorable reputation.

Charles and Carrie's marital bliss did not last long after their marriage in 1905. Although Carrie became pregnant shortly after the marriage, she had already begun living separately from her husband. A healthy baby girl was delivered in the spring of 1906.

In early June 1906, Carrie and Charles appeared before the court. Charles had been arrested for failing to provide for his family and was incarcerated from June 9 to 11. He was ordered by the court to pay $3 (around $600 today) per week in child support.

Charles and Carrie reunited after he was released from the Lawrence County jail, but their reunion was not going to be peaceful. In fact, it would lead to death for both of them.

A storm struck the area on Monday, June 10, 1907, just a year after Charles's release from jail. Hailstones pounded the home of the Shafers. One stone broke a pane out of their windows.

Charles noticed the broken pane two days later, on Wednesday. He quickly blamed young Hershel, who was eight years old. Carrie made attempts to explain about the storm and how the window became broken. Charles refused to believe her. He viciously began whipping Hershel. Empowered by a mother's love, Carrie rushed at Charles, trying to protect her son. Charles easily knocked her to the ground.

The family's neighbors could not ignore the sounds coming from the Shafers' home. They sent for the local law. Charles was once again arrested.

Alex South, constable of South Point, was responsible for arresting Charles. At first, Charles was taken to South's house on Greasy Ridge. Later, Charles was taken in handcuffs to Sybene. In Sybene, Charles was turned over to John Ellis, Charles's brother-in-law.

Rather than being comforted by her husband's arrest, Carrie was made more afraid. She feared retribution once Charles was released. She decided to go to her mother's house with Hershel and her infant daughter.

Carrie was right to be worried. Charles was not incarcerated for long. Shortly after being relinquished to Ellis, Charles either was released or escaped the same morning of his arrest.

Regardless of how he gained his freedom, Charles was free and angry. He had made a plan while in cuffs. Once free, he began to implement his plan.

First, Charles left Lawrence County, Ohio. He crossed the Ohio River and made his way to Huntington, West Virginia. In Huntington, he headed straight to the Emmons-Hawkins Hardware Company. It was there he purchased a single-barrel shotgun, a cartridge belt and two boxes of shotgun shells. A fifty-dollar bill was exchanged for his purchases. Once his change was given, Charles began his trip back to Lawrence County.

He crossed the Ohio River around 11:00 a.m. Then Charles followed the main road to Egerton Hill, where he entered the woods. Once concealed within the woods, he stopped to practice using his new gun.

Emmons-Hawkins Hardware Company. *Author's collection.*

When he was satisfied with his mastering of the gun, his travels began again. He was supposed to face the judge that afternoon. His wife would not miss the opportunity to betray him. Charles had already chosen the perfect spot to ambush his unsuspecting wife. James Yates's home was along the route his wife should use to get to court. Near Rockwood, Ohio, he settled in to wait just one hundred yards from the house. His presence was hidden by the brush.

Carrie's mother, Susan Payne Brammer Thacker, had grown tired of the treatment her daughter and grandchildren had received at the hands of Charles Shafer. She took action to stop the abuse for good. She swore out a warrant for Charles on Monday, June 11 for cruelty and beating her daughter. Squire Wilson Pritchard of Sybene issued the order.

Around noon on June 13, Susan, Carrie, Hershel and Carrie's infant daughter boarded a one-horse buggy and made their way to town. Mrs. Thacker handled the reins while Carrie held her daughter in her arms. Hershel sat between the two women. Like Charles expected, they chose the route that led them past James Yates's house. A fateful choice. One they would regret.

When Charles heard the buggy loaded with his family approaching, he jumped from behind the bushes that concealed him. Carrie was the first to see him. She could see the shotgun in his hands as well as the belt loaded with shells.

Knowing Charles's presence could lead only to her death, Carrie leaped from the carriage with her daughter in her arms. She was quickly followed

Thacker House. *Author's collection.*

by Hershel and her mother. They headed as quickly as possible for the safety of the Yates home.

The crack of the shotgun firing pierced the air. Carrie fell to the ground with a bullet in her stomach. She had to watch helplessly as her son and mother ran toward the house.

Susan had nearly reached the safety of the house when another shot rang out. This time she was struck. Mrs. Thacker fell to the ground. Thankfully, she was not struck in a vital place, but she may have not realized it at that moment.

Believing Susan dead, Charles ignored her fallen body to follow Hershel. James Yates had heard the commotion outside his home. A local tin typist and owner of a photo gallery, James was not prepared for what he was witnessing. Still, he rushed from the safety of his home to help the eight-year-old boy.

Hershel finally reached the porch. Yates was reaching to help him when Charles thrust his gun in James's face. He warned James not to interfere.

Before James could act, Charles grabbed Hershel by the arm. He dragged his son across Yates's yard to the road. Along the way, Hershel passed his grandmother's inert form. Then, he neared his bleeding mother. As they walked, Charles calmly reloaded his shotgun.

From the ground where she had fallen, Carrie begged for mercy for her son. Painfully, she raised herself from the road to plead with her husband to spare her son. James could see the agony on her face even from a distance. She used her last strength to try to protect her son.

Charles's response was quick but far from painless. With no expression on his face, he calmly listened to Carrie's pleas. He kept one hand on Hershel's arm while he placed the shotgun against Carrie's stomach. And he fired. His wife collapsed against the road. Her dying moans could be heard by those left to mourn her.

With his wife dying, Charles showed no emotion as he continued to drag the boy he helped raise. Into the woods the father and son went. The woods were so dense and thick that Charles and Hershel disappeared from sight.

Five minutes passed. A shot rang out. Screams from the boy echoed from the woods. Then, silence fell.

The youngest member of the Shafer family lay forgotten by almost all. Only a few months old, the tiny daughter born to Carrie and Charles lay in her mother's arms. She had been traveling in her mother's arms in the buggy when the shooting began. As her own father sought to kill his entire family, her mother used quick action to conceal the baby from Charles. Even as her grandmother, mother and brother were being shot without mercy, the baby was cradled next to her mother's body. Carrie realized her daughter's only hope was remaining invisible to her father. Thanks to her mother, the infant remained unharmed.

After the shot rang out from the woods, help began to arrive. Carrie and Susan were brought into the Yates home. In broken sentences, Carrie informed them of her daughter's presence. Her confession occurred an hour after the original shooting. Rescuers were happy to find the baby unharmed. As she waited for the doctor, Carrie asked to see her baby one more time. Once presented a final time to her mother, the baby was moved to the Nickols home nearby.

Dr. Gerlach and Dr. Morrison were summoned to assist Carrie and her mother. Mrs. Thacker had been shot in her shoulder. Although a flesh wound, the injury still caused concern.

Officers Brice and King were the first lawmen to arrive on the scene. Constable Frank Forgey arrived around twenty minutes after the shooting. The peace officers sent for the bloodhounds employed by the Ashland, Kentucky police.

As they waited for further assistance, those who were not aiding Carrie and her mother went searching for Hershel. The path left by his dragged body made its location easily discovered. The boy was discovered in a pool of his own blood and lying on his stomach. Two gaping wounds gave evidence of the cause of his death. Scorch marks on his coat around his wounds told how close the gun was when it fired into his small body. His face, distorted in pain and fear, gave witness to the horrors he faced in his last moments. The body was surrounded by debris, leaving people to believe Charles had wanted to set fire to the boy's body. For reasons known only to his murderer, Hershel's body was not ablaze.

His lifeless body was taken to the Hicks home on the Egerton property. No doubt his body was kept separate from his mother and grandmother in hopes to reduce their emotional pain.

A search party was formed to track Charles in the woods where he fled. The armed posse consisted of one hundred to two hundred men, all determined to bring the murderer to justice. Among the posse members was Officer Paffenbarger, who was in charge of the bloodhounds. The men searched Egerton Hill and circled back to Coryville, near present-day Proctorville. They tracked Charles as he traveled toward Bear Creek, then toward Braderick. From Braderick, they returned to Bear Creek before moving on to Charles's brother's home.

One hour and twenty minutes after the shooting, Carrie succumbed to her injuries. Her last words were said through clenched teeth.

"My boy is dead. I know. I heard the shot. I am dying. Charlie killed me. All the suffering I ever had, he caused." With these words, Carrie Brammer Shafer's life ended.

Susan Thacker was returned to her home that evening. She was still in serious condition.

The posse continued to search for Charles. Even as night fell, they searched. By surrounding the woods, they made sure Charles would not be able to escape them for long.

Squire B.C. Brammer was brought in to perform the postmortem on Carrie and Hershel. The gruesome task was made more difficult because the squire was an uncle of Carrie's.

The posse continued to search into the following morning. As the day began, Charles's body was discovered by the posse only a mile from the crime scene. Unable to escape, Charles had chosen to take his life rather than face the law. Lying in the weeds, Charles's weapon was by his side. An empty bottle of carbolic acid was held in a death grip of his corpse. Upon examination, they were surprised to discover he had died shortly before his body was found. The cause of death was listed as strychnine poisoning.

Carrie and Hershel were given a combined funeral at the little church in Rockwood, Lawrence County, Ohio. The mother and son were laid to rest together in the same grave in the family cemetery.

Susan Thacker struggled to recover from her injuries. Even though the wound appeared to be fairly minor, the infection it brought proved to be fatal. Susan Payne Brammer Thacker died of blood poisoning on June 21, 1907.

Charles's mother, Tacy Shafer, was arrested for a brief time. Although she was sixty years old, lawmen thought she had helped her son in his escape and was complicit in the crime. She was later released and did not face any official charges.

The Shafer Tragedy, as it was later called, drew attention as far away as Washington, D.C.

6

FROM FREEDOM TO SLAVERY

The Polley Kidnapping Case

The Polley case took nearly two hundred years before it was resolved. A grave injustice was committed in Lawrence County, Ohio, that time refused to forget.

Long before Kentucky became a state, slavery had a role in its history. Settlers moving into the uncharted territory brought slaves with them.

In 1833, Kentucky passed a nonimportation law. This law prohibited anyone from bringing people into the state for the purpose of selling them. That did not mean people could not enslave people or bring them with them when they moved to Kentucky. Slaveholders had to agree not to sell the people they held in bondage. By passing this law, the government of Kentucky had hoped to limit slavery within its borders.

Sadly, the law was repealed in 1849. The Constitutional Convention featured a debate on how to gradually allow for emancipation. The delegates were unsuccessful. The proslavery forces were just too powerful. Instead of limiting slavery, the Constitution strengthened the power of the slave owners.

Unlike many of the southern states, Kentucky was more lenient toward the people enslaved within its borders. For instance, there were no laws prohibiting teaching slaves to read or write. The state never forbade slaveholders from freeing their enslaved laborers. Freed slaves were also not forced to leave the state upon manumission like in Virginia.

These laws and rules did not prevent slavery in the state. In 1800, the tax records show seventy thousand slaves lived in Kentucky. By 1830, 24 percent of the population was enslaved.

The Polley case began in this period in Kentucky history. In 1837, a slaveholder in Pike County, Kentucky, wrote his will. David Pauley and his wife, Elizabeth, had owned slaves for years prior to 1837. Married on March 21, 1785, in Pittsylvania, Virginia, the Pauleys lived on fifty acres on the waters of Red Creek around three miles from Pikeville.

According to the 1830 Federal Census, the Pauley household consisted of ten people. Four were free white people, including one white male between the ages of sixty and sixty-nine (which would be David); one white female between the ages of five and nine; one white female between the ages of thirty and thirty-nine; and one white female between the ages of sixty and sixty-nine (which would be Elizabeth). There were also six slaves: two males under the age of five; one male between the age of ten and twenty-three; two males between the ages of twenty-four and thirty-five; and one male between thirty-six and fifty-four.

At some time in his life, David became conflicted about slavery. Times were changing, and so were people's thoughts about slavery. David seemed to be changing his mind about slavery and his ownership of other people. When he wrote his will, he chose to free his slaves upon his death.

When his will was transcribed, David's decision became known. People, including his wife, were not happy with his decision. Since David was still alive, they knew they had a chance to change his mind.

His wife, Elizabeth, was successful in postponing his decision. When she died in 1839, her death prompted the conditions of his will to be changed. It could be argued that these changes were more beneficial to those under the yoke of slavery.

In August 1847, David Pauley passed away and his will was read. Not only had he freed those he had enslaved, but his entire estate, including land and money, would be theirs as well.

Seven people were to benefit from David's generosity. The seven were siblings and named Dug, Peyton, John, Spencer, Jude, Mirah and William.

Of course, David's family immediately contested the will. There was no way they would allow these formerly enslaved people to take what they assumed would be theirs. After much debate and conversations, a compromise was reached. The manumitted slaves agreed to relinquish all claims to the money and land in exchange for their freedom.

To honor David's decision, Peyton and his six siblings chose to take the Pauley name. However, they did change the spelling from Pauley to Polley.

Without their inheritance, the Polleys had no money to leave Pike County, Kentucky. Not only did they wish to move to Ohio, but they also had family members still in the bonds of slavery. Specifically, they wanted to free Peyton's wife, Violet, and his children. The children included fifteen-year-old Dugel, thirteen-year-old Dayton, ten-year-old Harrison, eight-year-old Nelson and four-year-old Aaron. It would take no small feat to reach their goals. The family hired themselves out for work. By working odd jobs for numerous people, they slowly built a nest egg. It took them two years, but they succeeded in saving enough to free Violet and ten of the children.

Violet and the children were the property of David and Nancy Pauley Campbell. As you might have guessed, they were related to David Pauley. Nancy was David and Elizabeth's adult daughter. David Campbell was their son-in-law.

Campbell was not the successful man his father-in-law was. He was well known for making bad business decisions. Part of his problem was that he had a drinking problem. He may have even been a full-fledged alcoholic. Campbell did not just drink alcohol: he was a bootlegger as well. He was arrested and faced fines for his illegal activities numerous times. All of these problems led him and Nancy to be heavily in debt.

Campbell had many creditors. All were worried that they would never see their money again. When they heard of Campbell selling eleven slaves, they rushed to collect as much money as they could.

David Campbell met his creditors with a lie. He informed them that Dug and Peyton had not paid cash to purchase the freedom of their family. He said they had given him a promissory note.

Why did the creditors believe the lie? It seems unlikely that anyone, much less a white slaveholder, would have accepted a promissory note from former slaves. Since Dug and Peyton had been free for less than three years, why would someone trust them to pay off their debt? They did have a witness. Joseph Fulkerson stood as witness to the sale.

Maybe the creditors did not believe David Campbell at all. Perhaps they saw the former slaves as a better way to collect what they were owed. They clearly knew Campbell was not the best bet.

The community also knew the Polley family's plan. After Peyton had rescued Violet and their children from slavery, the Polleys planned to leave for the freedom of Ohio in the spring of 1849.

The Campbells' many creditors knew time was of the essence. They needed to move quickly. So they declared the sale of Violet and the children a scam. They claimed Campbell was using a fraudulent sale to keep from paying their debt. They chose to sue both David Campbell and the newly

Map of Pike County, Kentucky. *Author's collection.*

freed, hardworking Polley family. The Polleys knew they were going to be fighting an uphill battle with little chance of winning. Dug used some of their hard-earned money to pay the creditors $400. Another $150 had to be paid by Dug for fines.

Even after paying $550 dollars, the Polleys were not able to satisfy all the debt collectors. These remaining debts would break apart their happy family once again.

First, the Polleys would have to leave someone behind in Pike County, Kentucky. Someone had to stand in as a promise for them to return and pay the rest of the debt. Peyton and Violet's oldest son, Nathan, was the one chosen to remain behind. George Brown kept Nathan in his possession until he worked off the debt or his family returned to pay it off.

The court case delayed the Polleys from leaving for Ohio by a few months. With some sadness for leaving Nathan behind, they left in June 1849. Their travels would be far from easy.

At the mouth of the Big Sandy River, the Polley family was once again facing a major obstacle. Another creditor of David Campbell had appeared. He refused to allow the Polleys to proceed any further without satisfying the $61.55 debt. The Polleys had already spent most of their money paying Campbell's other debts. They had no more money left.

True freedom was so close, yet so far away. Ohio was their dream: a place where they could not only be free, but they might actually escape slavery forever as well.

With no way to pay the debt and Ohio so close, the only solution left was to leave behind another family member. Once again the Polleys chose to ask a son to stay behind. Douglas, the second-eldest son, remained behind until the debt was repaid.

On July 1, 1849, the Polley family crossed the Ohio River into Lawrence County, Ohio. They quickly registered their manumission papers with the county clerk. To finance their new beginning, they found work as field hands on local farms.

Just a few days after their arrival, Dug set out to reunite part of their family. He traveled back to the Big Sandy area to pay the debt and obtain Douglas's release. Once he arrived in Ohio, Douglas found a job to pay off his bounty.

Only one family member was missing: Nathan. Just one month after arriving in Ohio, Dug left the family behind and returned to Pike County, Kentucky. He paid $125 to free Nathan. Finally, the family was whole again.

The Polleys settled in Perry Township, Lawrence County, Ohio. Peyton and Violet purchased land along Little Ice Creek. Described as industrious by their new neighbors, they built a comfortable new home to raise their family.

It was a Hollywood happy ending, but their story was not over. What happened next would make ripples in history and time that would be felt over one hundred years later.

On June 6, 1850, nine of Peyton and Violet's children were kidnapped from their house in Burlington. "A band of devils" raided the Polley home. Although the names of the kidnappers were not recorded, they were reportedly from Lawrence County, Ohio, and Kentucky. Nine of the Polley children were grabbed from their slumber, dragged out of their home and forced to cross the Ohio River. Once across the Ohio, the children were sold into slavery.

A neighbor said Violet's wails of grief would echo in his mind for years after the horrible event.

Immediately, Lawrence Countians joined together to save the Polley children. Ralph Leete and a Mr. Watson were some of the first to pursue the kidnappers. Leete was the prosecuting attorney for Lawrence County, Ohio. Watson was from Catlettsburg, Kentucky. Though quick on the kidnapped children's trail, Leete and Watson were unable to apprehend the kidnappers before the children were sold.

The children were split into two groups. Four were sold to a Virginian. Five were taken to Maysville, Kentucky, to be sold.

Leete may have not been able to overcome the kidnappers before they sold the children, but he had not given up recovering them. He pursued them.

The five children who made it to Maysville, Kentucky, found themselves further separated. Four of the five were sent overland from Maysville to Louisville, Kentucky. Once in Louisville, the plan was to ship the children farther into the Deep South on steamboats.

Leete and Lester D. Walton had continued to chase the Polleys and their captors. Their search began in Lawrence County, Kentucky. On the farm of David Justice located on the Tug Fork branch of the Big Sandy River near Maynard, Kentucky, they received their first clues to the children's whereabouts. Their focus was on Jamie McMillian and William Squire Ratcliffe.

Jamie McMillian was the man who was transporting the four through Kentucky. Leete and Walton had thought they were having success when they caught a steamboat bound for Maysville, Kentucky. Sadly, the children were not on board.

Leete and Walton did not give up. They learned the children had been turned over to the Lewis Robards Slave Trading Company in Lexington, Kentucky. At the trading company, the two men learned one of the children had been auctioned off to slaveholders in Louisville, one had been sold to a local farm in Lexington and one child had been sold to a tobacco farm near Frankfort, Kentucky. Another child was located in Frankfort, Kentucky, but more specifics were not recorded. A final child had been located in Shelbyville, Kentucky.

Leete had to call on his legal expertise to assist in freeing the children. The five in Kentucky included twenty-one-year-old Hulda, sixteen-year-old Peyton Jr., ten-year-old Martha and four-year-old Mary Jane. Mary Jane was not only the youngest child but also the only Polley to be born free in Ohio.

His first step was to file a case in each city where one of the children had been located. Four separate cases were required. Leete was successful in pleading his case. The children were ordered to be returned to their parents. To ensure their safety, they were escorted back to Lawrence County, Ohio, by the U.S. Army.

William Squire Ratcliffe had purchased the other four Polley children. Nelson, Harrison, Louisa and Anna Polley were the children sold in Virginia. Once Ratcliffe made his purchase, he took the children across the Tug Fork to his home in Wayne County, Virginia. After 1863, this county became part of the newly created state of West Virginia.

The children who were transported to Virginia were the first to be located but the last to be freed. Ralph Leete and Lester Walton filed claims in Guyandotte, Virginia, attempting to free the children almost immediately.

The children were sold to Ratcliffe in 1851. Three years would pass before they won their freedom in the Cabell County Courts.

Ratcliffe was not going to give up his property lightly. He appealed the case, claiming the Cabell County Courts did not have the appropriate jurisdiction to even hear the case. According to him, the case needed to be held in Wayne County, Virginia, where he lived.

Sadly, one of the children died the following year. Nelson Polley, who had been freed in 1849, died enslaved in 1855.

The Polley case was claiming attention from all across the country.

In 1852, Governor Reuben Wood of Ohio paid special attention to the case. He requested inquiries be conducted by the General Assembly. Wood gave permission for anything to be done to ensure the children's release. He agreed to pay for any of Leete's expenses with the assembly's contingency fund.

The General Assembly gave the governor their report. The case in Kentucky was pending, but the outcome looked promising. The Virginia case was another story. They reported there were too many difficulties to provide assistance in the West Virginia case.

Ohio's governor was not the only one taking action. Kentucky's Governor Crittenden issued warrants for the arrest of the kidnappers. However, some of the warrants were never served. It seems the enforcement of the governor's orders was

Governor Reuben Wood. *Author's collection.*

a problem. Just another example of Kentucky being split by proslavery proponents and abolitionists.

A new case was filed in the Wayne County, Virginia courts to free the remaining four Polleys in bondage. John Laidley was the one chosen to file the complaint. His task was not easy, to say the least.

The Polley case in Virginia became more problematic because of their enslaver. William Squire Ratcliffe was no ordinary slaveholder. He had an abundance of political power within his community. He was not surrendering without a fight. He used his influence to keep the case from going to trial. He could not lose the case if it was never tried. He was doing everything to make sure he got his way.

The last record of the Polley case in Virginia's courts was in 1859. The case was marked unresolved at that time.

Of course, a major historical event changed the case's path forever. The American Civil War began. The country was torn apart. The Polley case took a back seat to a national crisis.

That does not mean the Polley case had been forgotten. Far from it. Leete still looked for ways to find justice for the four Polley children enslaved in Virginia.

Ralph Leete recommended the State of Ohio hire George W. Summers. As Summers was a resident of Kanawha County, Virginia (later West Virginia), Leete felt Summers would be more successful than he would be. So Summers was hired in 1859.

The case caught the attention of the most important person in America. President Abraham Lincoln summoned Ralph Leete to the White House. He had heard of the travesty that had befallen the Polley family. He wanted to learn more. Many believe the Polleys' case may have inspired the Emancipation Proclamation.

When Ohio senator John Bingham authored the Thirteenth, Fourteenth and Fifteenth Amendments of the U.S. Constitution, he would look toward the Polley case. He studied the case before and while writing the amendments.

Governor Wood was still fighting to help the children. General Joel W. Wilson of Tiffin, Ohio, was appointed by the governor as the counsel on behalf of the children in 1860. His pay would come from the State of Ohio.

In the end, the Civil War brought freedom that courts could not. The Polley children all returned home as the war drew to a close—all except Nelson, who had died in bondage.

One may wonder why the children and their benefactors would have such difficulty in obtaining their freedom. The laws of the period made obtaining freedom extremely difficult for freed slaves who were once again enslaved. The freedmen found in a slave state had to prove they had a right to freedom.

As for slaves found in free states, the enslaved had to be returned to their owners. In fact, people could face fines and incarceration if they resisted turning a slave back to those who claimed ownership.

Ohio would spend over $3,000 trying to free the Polley children in Virginia.

One may wonder what caused the Polley family to suffer such a tragedy. Was it merely chance, or were they specifically targeted?

They were targeted. This tragedy was the idea of two greedy men. David Campbell, Violet's former owner, was still dealing with his many debts. He was not willing to work hard and settle his debts himself. He wanted to take a shortcut. That shortcut would lead to the longest-running fugitive slave case in U.S. history.

David Campbell found an ally in a man named David Justice. Justice was a slave catcher, one of the many men who hunted people down like animals to sell them back to their owners. Campbell convinced Justice he still owned the children. With Justice's seizure of the children, a $1,000 debt would be satisfied.

The Polley family tragedy made national news once again in 2012. On April 6, 2012, Judge Darrell Pratt of Wayne County, West Virginia's Circuit Court entered a decree declaring the Polley children were wrongfully kidnapped. He further went on to declare Harrison, Louisa and Anna Polley "were and are free persons as of March 22, 1859."

Long delayed and nearly forgotten, the Polley family found justice.

7

THE MYSTERIOUS DEATH
OF AVANELLE SMITH

At 2:00 p.m. on Saturday, May 11, 1963, a startling sight was beheld by Leo Hawthorne and his nephew Jack Hawthorne. The two were traveling on Indian Guyan Road, and their original destination was Oscar Sloan's house. Just five miles northeast of Chesapeake, Ohio, in a dry streambed near Indian Guyan Creek, Leo and Jack saw the body of a woman. It was obvious she was long deceased.

Leo did not stop to investigate further but hurried to the home of Deputy Sheriff Harold Johnson of Chesapeake. Harold was another nephew of Leo's. Leo knew his discovery needed to be reported right away. Of course, in 1963, contacting the authorities was not as simple as making a cellphone call. In fact, not everyone in the county could claim to own a telephone within their home. For Leo, getting help meant driving to his nephew's home.

Deputy Johnson and Deputy Joe Akers returned to the scene with Leo. What they found was quite shocking. A partially decomposed, nude body of a woman lay in the ravine.

The two deputies began to assess the situation and looked for clues to the woman's identity. It was estimated she was five feet, five inches tall, and weighed around 130 pounds. No clothing could be found on or near the body.

Her identity was hard to determine because her body had been exposed to the elements and wild animals. Her face was partially gone. Animals appeared to have eaten her shoulder and part of her arm.

Lying on her back, it did not look like she had been shot. Later examinations would show that she had been strangled.

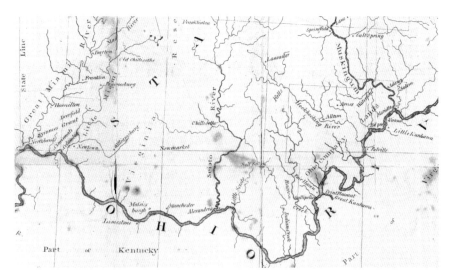

Map of Indian Guyan River. *Author's collection.*

While other people processed the crime scene, Deputies Johnson and Akers traveled to the nearest house. Oscar Sloan's house was just three hundred feet from the ravine. Leo and Jack had been heading there before their discovery sent them to Deputy Harold Johnson's home.

At Sloan's house, the deputies found much to investigate. First, they found a still, mash and whiskey in the house. Federal agents took Oscar into custody for having an illegal still. However, Oscar was too intoxicated to give any information about the body found so close to his home.

Two women were also found in the Sloan house. One was Oscar's wife, Thelma Sloan. The second was Hazel Nemeth. Both women were taken into custody.

A resident of Huntington, West Virginia, and North Kenova, Ohio, Hazel had been in the Sloan house for days. Like Oscar, she was horribly intoxicated. Later, the police would discover she had walked up the path near the body on Friday evening.

Inside the house, the deputies found more questions than answers. With two of the house's inhabitants intoxicated, they were forced to look for information in other ways. Pools of dried blood were found inside and outside the house. A small, bloodstained rug had been thrown in the yard. The rug lay suspiciously beside an axe.

With all the evidence coming in from different places, it was up to Sheriff Carl E. Ross and his deputies to solve the mystery of the woman's identity and catch her killer.

Three different doctors examined the body. Pathologist Dr. S. Werthammer was brought in to perform the autopsy. Pathologist Dr. J. Evan Saddler of Huntington was also given credit for performing the autopsy. His procedure took place at the Huntington Hospital on Sunday, May 12, 1963. Dr. Nenni, however, gave the statement of what the autopsies uncovered.

According to Dr. Nenni, the body was of a woman thirty to thirty-five years of age. She had reddish-brown hair and stood five feet, three inches. She weighed 110 pounds. The doctors also stated the woman appeared to have never given birth. The cause of death was still not confirmed. The woman's neck tissue had been subject to animals and the elements. The doctors believed she had been strangled but could not say for sure.

Their next step was to identify the body. Sheriff Ross summoned the Bureau of Identification and Criminal Investigation of London, Ohio. They arrived in Lawrence County, Ohio, on May 12 and completed their investigation on May 13.

They took her fingerprints. Luckily, they were able to conclude the unidentified woman was Avanelle Smith. The identity was confirmed on May 14, 1963, three days after her remains were found. Arnold Fetter, a former Irontonian, was given credit for matching the fingerprints.

Avanelle was forty-seven years old and a resident of Proctorville, Ohio. She lived in a trailer there with her husband, Raymond Smith. She was a mother of two children: Willard Ray Smith and Codine Smith Lake.

Some of the pathologists' findings did not match Avanelle. First, she was over twelve years older than they had estimated. Second, she had given birth twice. The doctors did state that it was possible that because Avanelle had given birth so long ago, it was not apparent in the autopsy.

Avanelle's husband was questioned by police, who hoped he could shed some light on what happened to his wife. According to Raymond, Avanelle had left their home on May 4. She had not been seen since. He had not called the police because it was not unusual for Avanelle to stay away from home for short periods of time.

Avanelle's murder garnered attention from communities across the tristate. Cabell County, West Virginia's Sheriff Harold Frankel was the one to find articles of clothing believed to be Avanelle's.

After Avanelle's body was examined, her remains were transported to the Schneider Funeral Home in Chesapeake, Ohio. Just a few days after her remains were identified, graveside services were held for those who wanted to say their final farewells to Avanelle. Avanelle Smith's body was laid to rest in Union Hill Cemetery, Chesapeake, Ohio.

The Sloan house was still being investigated. The blood found on the rug and in the four-roomed house could have been from either a deer or a person. The investigators did discover a deer had been killed in the vicinity recently. Samples of the blood were sent to a lab for more information.

A private road leads from the Sloan house to a spot seventy-five feet from Avanelle's remains.

Thelma and Oscar Sloan were finally sober. They were questioned by the police over and over again on May 13. Both claimed to have no knowledge of Avanelle or why her body was found so close to their home.

Both Oscar and Thelma Sloan remained in police custody. They were being charged with a liquor violation for running an illegal still.

On May 17, 1963, the Federal Bureau of Investigation joined local law enforcement to solve the case. No new developments had been found. One day prior, the clothing found by Sheriff Frankel had been turned over to Sheriff Ross.

On May 22, 1963, a grand jury was called. No specific person was targeted by the jury's investigation. In the end, the jury stated the case required more investigation before going to court.

Sheriff Ross and Dr. Nenni vowed to continue trying to solve the mystery of Avanelle Smith.

8

ALL FOR LOVE

Dueling Women

On a quiet spring Sunday evening, the peace of one Lawrence County community was shattered by a duel. Two people fell in love with the same person and were determined to prove their strong feelings even if they might die.

In most cases, duelists were men, but not in 1889. In the small community of Athalia in Rome Township, Lawrence County, Ohio, the Sunday evening services had ended. Residents began to make their way back to their homes. Two young women met to settle a disagreement once and for all.

Betty Kyle and Julia Rucker were being courted by the same man. He had been secretly seeing both young women while they remained unaware they had competition. When they learned of his betrayal, they chose to attack each other instead of the man who had wronged them.

At first, Betty and Julia used words to argue back and forth. Jealousy charged the argument. At first, the girls' friends tried to intercede, but they quickly realized they could not stop the fight.

Soon words were not enough. The girls drew pocketknives from their Sunday best. Onlookers no longer were willing to risk physical harm to stop the two women.

The fight was oddly quiet. The women did not yell, scream or moan. No words were spoken as they swung the knives at each other.

Julia tried to flee the fight at one point. She ran for fifty to sixty yards, but Betty was hard on her tail.

Houses in Athalia. *Author's collection.*

The violent fight ended when Betty Kyle fell to the ground. Upon inspection, she had suffered eighteen cuts during the altercation. Two or three cuts were near her spine. One cut ran from her spine to her left forearm. A few of her injuries appeared to be fatal. Her extensive injuries caused her to faint from blood loss.

As for her opponent, Julia had not escaped the fight uninjured. She, too, had multiple cuts and injuries. Unlike Betty, Julia did not have any serious injuries.

Betty was taken for treatment while Julia was taken into custody. Justice Bowen was called to hear the case. Julia claimed self-defense. After hearing the evidence from witnesses and Julia, Bowen dismissed the case.

The two women, however, made the news across the country. Newspapers as far away as Pittsburgh, Pennsylvania, carried the story. Of course, the articles made a few mistakes. For instance, one article claimed Betty's last name was Bowen, not Kyle. Regardless, Julia and Betty's unladylike behavior gained them some notoriety.

Thankfully, Betty did not succumb to her vast injuries. Not only did no obituary appear for Betty, but it also appeared that she married that fall. Did she win the heart of her beau? No one quite knows. The beau's name was never mentioned in any of the articles about the duel.

As for Julia, no records of her appeared at all. No obituary. No census records. Absolutely nothing. Did the newspapers use the wrong surname for her as well? Or was she just visiting the area? Since no more information can be found, what happened to Julia is unknown.

9

THE SAFECRACKERS

At 3:00 a.m. on May 24, 1889, the early morning silence was shattered by an explosion. The east end of Ironton was rattled as the safe at Jacob Meyers's saloon was blown open. Located on the northeast corner of Second and Madison Streets in Ironton, the saloon had been closed for hours.

Jacob Meyers and his family had been sleeping peacefully above his saloon when the explosion rocked his home and business. At that time, Jacob and his wife, Mary, shared their home with their two sons, Charles and Joseph.

Born around 1839 in Wurttemberg, Germany, Jacob not only owned a saloon but also brewed his own beer. His son Charles had begun assisting in the family brewery and saloon. The brewery was relatively small; it had not even been noted in the local city directories or newspapers.

On that early morning, three men had entered Meyers's saloon with the intention of wreaking havoc. The men drilled a hole in the saloon's safe. They then shoved an abundance of gunpowder into the hole. The concussion from the blast blew the safe's door off its hinges, broke several windows and scattered items around the room.

Meyers emerged from his apartment above the saloon to a scene of chaos. His bar was filled with smoke, but the thieves were nowhere to be seen. When he explored further, Jacob discovered the thieves had stolen $75 (or $2,060 today) from him.

The three men had caught the notice of more than one local resident. Meyers and his neighbors had seen three men hanging around the saloon for

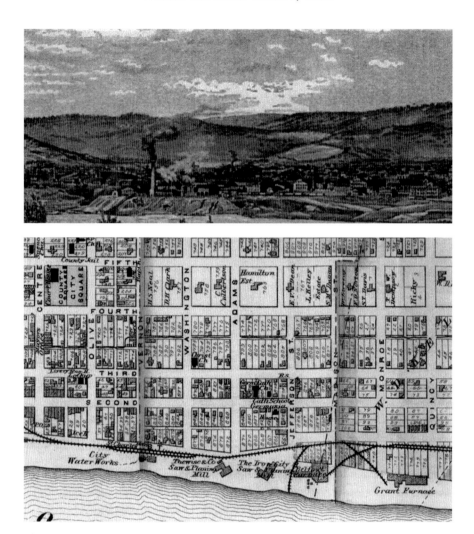

Top: Ironton, Ohio, in 1887. *Author's collection.*

Bottom: Map of Madison Street in Ironton, Ohio, circa 1877 *Author's collection.*

a few days prior to the explosion. They had been casing the saloon, getting ready to make their move.

Earlier in the evening, the same three men were spotted near Pirring's Stable. They caught the notice of residents because of their suspicious actions. The three had been sleeping in the stable located near the Iron Railroad Tunnel on Friday evening.

The witnesses had similar descriptions of the men. They were described as smart-looking, meaning they were well dressed. Although well dressed,

Big Etna Furnace. *Author's collection.*

they were also rough and tough. Two of the men had solemn expressions, but the third had a sickly smile.

Their arrival in town had been noted. The train conductor who had brought them into town had warned the police to watch them. Coming from somewhere west of Chillicothe, they were trouble on legs.

After the theft, Conductor Critzer of the Detroit, Toledo and Ironton Railroad saw the men trying to leave the county. The men had boarded the train at Big Etna Furnace and left it at Wellston, Jackson County, Ohio. He reported the information to Marshal Vanhorn of Ironton.

Believing they were on the right track, Marshal Vanhorn and Officer Clark traveled to Wellston. When they apprehended the three men, they still had $50 of the $75 they had stolen in the form of scorched paper money as well as silver coins. A steel saw and file gave evidence of their crime. Meyers was far from the first of their victims.

Vanhorn and Clark took the men into their custody and brought them back to Ironton to face the consequences of their actions.

On June 7, 1889, the three men were arraigned before the common pleas court. Identified as John Slavens, George W. Souder and James W. Martin, the three men made a notable entrance into the courtroom.

John Slavins, alias John Cavanaugh, was twenty-nine years old and no stranger to the law. Standing at five feet, nine inches tall, John was the shortest of the men. He had deep blue eyes and a fair complexion. His dark brown hair seemed to conflict with his red beard. When asked, he claimed he worked as a farmer. John had multiple tattoos. On his left forearm, he had five-pointed stars below two flags. Another pair of flags appeared on his right forearm with an eagle above it. Lastly, he had a tattoo of a woman standing with a hoop in her hand on his left arm.

Like Slavins, George W. Souder was not the most upstanding citizen. He used the alias Flemming. He was only twenty-three years old and had worked as a cigar maker. At six feet even, he had brown hair and a beard. George also had India ink tattoos. On his left forearm, he had a woman standing on tiptoe stretching her arms above her head. The initials F.F. were tattooed above a heart with a dagger through it on his right forearm.

The last burglar was James Willis. Also known as James Martin, he was the oldest of the trio at the ripe old age of thirty-four. He claimed he worked as a saloonkeeper and farmer. His medium dark complexion set off his murky blue eyes. His one tattoo was located on his left forearm.

Since all three men had more than one run-in with the law, their entrance into the courtroom seemed even more peculiar. The three men entered the courtroom using their handcuffed hands to cover their faces. Afraid the court photographer would take their picture, they refused to uncover their faces as they sat. They did spread their fingers to peek around the room.

Judge Davis was assigned to hear the case. He had trouble keeping everyone focused on the case at hand. Laughter filled the courtroom as the men hid behind their fingers.

The slightest movement startled John, George and James. Their nervous jolts did little to stop the laughter overflowing the room.

George W. Souder was the first to answer the court's questions. He was ordered to remove his hands from his face. Forced to comply, he removed one of his hands. That move did not help the situation because he kept one hand up over his face. George even spread his fingers of the remaining hand to replace the hand he had to lower.

John Hamilton had been appointed to represent John, George and James. Hamilton was far from being pleased. In fact, he told the court, "No, I'm not their lawyer and I don't want to be." Despite his protests, Judge Davis finalized Hamilton's appointment as the lawyer for the defense.

The trial was set for June 17, 1889. The men were sent back to jail.

The trial was destined to be short and sweet. Colonel Williams was chosen to represent the state. By 4:00 p.m., all the testimony had been given. The prosecutor and defense attorney gave their closing arguments. By 9:30 p.m., the jury had been sent away to deliberate.

Two days later, the jury had reached a verdict. They had made a decision by 4:00 a.m. At 9:00 a.m., the court was once again called to order. The jury foreman stood to pronounce the verdict: guilty of burglary and grand larceny.

Oddly, the three defendants seemed completely unaffected by the verdict. Hamilton asked permission to speak to his clients privately. The judge allowed them to use the vacated jury room. After five minutes, they returned to the courtroom.

The judge sentenced the men to seven years in the Ohio State Penitentiary. One of the men smiled. The other two men appeared relieved and a little contented.

John, George and James were escorted to the Ohio State Penitentiary on June 20, 1889. They would spend seven years there for burglary and larceny. All three would leave the prison on November 25, 1893.

Thus ended the Meyerses' explosive robbery.

10

BALLARD ROBBERS

*J*ohn Ballard had arrived in Lawrence County, Ohio, sometime between 1830 and 1840. He and his family settled on a farm three miles from South Point alongside Solida Creek in Fayette Township. Within ten years after arriving, the Ballard family suffered a devastating loss when John's first wife died. Her name, date of death and cause of death were not recorded in local registers. However, she left behind at least five small children.

On May 11, 1851, John married for the second time. His new wife was named Cassandra Rigg. She and John welcomed their first child, John M., within a year of their wedding. Three more children would follow.

John supported his family by farming on his land in Fayette Township, Lawrence County, Ohio. According to the 1860 census, his personal estate was worth $1,200 (around $43,000 today). His farm was valued at $2,600, or over $94,000 today. One of John's sons from his first marriage, Barton, was still living at home and working on the family farm as a laborer.

As it did for many families across the country, the Civil War changed the Ballard family drastically. John and Cassandra decided to begin anew. John began selling off their household goods as well as their property to make a move to Missouri. He stockpiled the resulting funds within his home. Some of the money had already been sent to Missouri as a down payment on their new home. Some $6,000 ($133,000 today) was stored safely in a box. Its location was known only to John and Cassandra.

John's actions captured the attention of people who decided to relieve the Ballards from their hard-earned money.

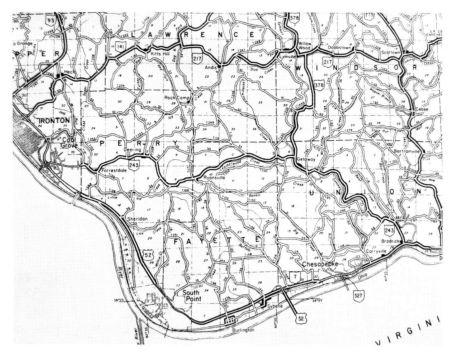

Map of Solida Creek. *Author's collection.*

It was around midnight on the family farm. John Ballard, his wife and their young children had settled in for a good night's rest. Just three miles from South Point on Solida Creek, the family slept peacefully, exhausted from their preparations for their move west.

A loud crash echoed through the home as five men broke down their door using a rail. Two men grabbed John from his bed. They dragged him out into the yard and began to beat him using their guns.

A terrified Mrs. Ballard was guarded by two of the remaining men. Forced to remain in bed while her husband was being brutally beaten, she quickly identified where the couple had hidden a box full of cash.

The remaining robber followed Cassandra's directions to the box of money; $6,000 had been hidden within the house. Their chance of a new beginning was being taken from them.

Once the men had what they wanted, the five men left the house. John Ballard lay in the yard nearly beaten to death. Cassandra and her eighteen-year-old son, John M., were left in shock and horror.

Even as they fled the scene, the thieves' chance of escape had already been reduced. Cassandra had, surprisingly, recognized two of the men. So had her son. Two of the robbers were John's sons from his first marriage: Isaac and Barton.

Known affectionately as Asa, Isaac was the oldest son born during John's first marriage. Isaac had worked on the family farm growing up. By 1860, he had left his father's home and was working as a farm laborer on the Hastings' farm. When the Civil War broke out, Isaac joined the Union army. He was described as a fair-haired, blue-eyed twenty-two-year-old man. Weighing 150 pounds, he stood five feet, eight inches. One notable flaw was that his eyes were crossed.

Like his older brother, Barton was also a Civil War veteran. Born on March 10, 1847, he was eleven years younger than Asa. He remained in the family home working by his father's side long after Isaac had left.

Since the sheriff knew the identity of two of the robbers, it did not take him long to capture the first of the thieves. Barton Ballard was the first one captured. His shoes proved his participation in the robbery of his father. Facing robbery and attempted murder charges, Barton quickly turned on his accomplices.

According to Barton, his brother Isaac was the ringleader. He and Barton asked their brother-in-law, William Walker, to join them in their criminal plans. Walker was only seventeen years old. Like Barton, he had light hair and blue eyes. Walker and Isaac would plan the attack together.

Realizing they could not be successful without more muscle, Walker and the Ballard brothers hired the Kelly brothers.

Charles Kelly was not unknown to local law enforcement. Like Barton and Isaac, he too had joined the army during the Civil War. Unlike the Ballard brothers, Charles deserted his military responsibilities. Charles also had a warrant out for his arrest from West Virginia for stealing horses. Standing five feet, eight inches tall, Charles weighed 125 pounds. Like the other men, he had a fair complexion and blue eyes. The brown-haired Charles had noticeable buck teeth. His unique appearance would play a role in his capture.

Believing they had the perfect partners in crime, Isaac and Walker promised the Kelly brothers $1,000 each to help rob Isaac's father and stepmother.

As for the rest of the robbers, the money would be split as evenly as possible. Walker would be paid $1,400. With $3,400 going to their partners, Barton and Isaac would split the remaining $2,600. Since Isaac was the leader, he may have been given a larger share than Barton, but that was not recorded at the time of their arrest.

WICKED LAWRENCE COUNTY, OHIO

Walker's brother-in-law Isaac Tonie was believed to have participated in the robbery. He was even arrested, but Barton quickly exonerated Tonie.

Although Barton was the first to be arrested, Walker and Jim Kelly were soon taken into custody. Barton, Walker and Jim were transported to the Ironton jail on October 5, 1968.

The three men's share of the ill-gotten money was recovered around the time of their arrest. Walker had done his best to keep his share hidden. He split the $1,400 and hid it in six different locations.

Isaac and Charles were not going down so quickly. A $200 reward was promised to anyone who could assist the local law enforcement officers in capturing the two men.

The two men fled over the nearby hills toward Burlington, Ohio. They planned to cross the Ohio River into West Virginia to escape capture.

Among the robbers, only Isaac had suffered an injury during the assault on John Ballad. While he was striking his father over the head multiple times with his revolver, the gun discharged. The bullet struck Isaac in his leg. According to Barton, his brother was severely wounded. Deputies hoped these injuries would make his capture easier. They were wrong.

Isaac would, however, have a few close encounters with the local law enforcement. At one point, he was surrounded while hiding on a local hilltop. His left arm had been hit twice. One shot wounded him just above his wrist and the other slightly above his elbow.

Isaac had loaded himself down with seven revolvers. He had no problem using them to escape capture.

While his son and Charles Kelly were leading the local officers on a chase across the southern Ohio hills, John Ballard was fighting for his life. On the Monday following the attack, John was still alive. Doctors had become hopeful for his recovery.

Despite his efforts to remain free, Isaac was eventually arrested on Sunday, October 18, 1868. Isaac had taken refuge on Cracker's Neck, a desolate and secluded part of Kentucky ninety miles from Ironton. T.C. Campbell and Noah Powers from Ironton were the ones to end Isaac's flight from justice.

Campbell and Powers had been searching for Ballard for quite some time. They traveled around two hundred miles in West Virginia and Kentucky in search of Isaac. Looking for more assistance, the two men hired a Mr. Rice and Mr. Webb on the Big Sandy River. They paid the men $100 each.

Rice had been searching for Isaac when a stroke of luck hit. He was in a general store in Cracker's Neck when Isaac Ballard walked in. Rice sprang into action and arrested Isaac.

Surprisingly, Isaac offered no resistance. Once Rice had him, the rest of the posse emerged from the bushes surrounding the store. Isaac's flight was finally over.

When questioned about the robbery, Isaac admitted to robbing his father. However, he claimed he had not harmed his father in any way. In his pockets, the posse found $565.

Isaac arrived in Lawrence County, Ohio, and was placed in the jail on October 21, 1868.

Charles Kelly remained at large.

Barton Ballard flipped on his brother and other accomplices. Since he turned state's evidence, Barton would serve four months in jail.

In February 1869, a reporter from the *Ironton Register* toured the Lawrence County jail. Walstein Kelly and the Ballard brothers were sharing the same "apartment" in the jail. The reporter found the men jolly and willing to answer any questions the reporter asked.

Walstein "Jim" Kelly would be found not guilty of robbery. He was released from the jail shortly after the reporter's visit. Like Barton, he would serve only four months for the attack on the Ballard farm.

Isaac Ballard and William Walker stood trial for robbery and attempted murder in May 1869. John S. George was appointed to prosecute the case. O.F. Moore, General Enochs and O.S. Collier represented the defendants. The jury found Walker and Isaac guilty. The two men were transferred to the Ohio Penitentiary on May 31, 1869. Walker would serve four years, while Isaac would serve five.

As for the Ballard family, they survived the frightful experience. Most of their savings were recovered. John and Cassandra were able to relocate to their new home near Urich, Henry County, Missouri. Decades later, Urich was described as a "delightful village, surrounded by a fertile county."

Casandra Rigg Ballard died on February 22, 1876. She was buried in Kepner Cemetery near her new home in Urich, Henry County, Missouri.

John Ballard lived three years longer than his wife. He died on September 18, 1879, just eleven years after surviving the brutal attack. He was buried beside Cassandra in Kepner Cemetery in Urich.

Before his father's death, Barton may have been able to make amends with his father. By 1870, he was working as a farm laborer near his family's new home in Missouri.

Isaac and Walstein would serve their prison sentences, and there the records stop.

As for Charles Kelly, he may have never faced justice for his crimes. The local newspapers are silent about what truly happened to him.

11

BADGER GAME

What, you may ask, is a badger game? It does not refer to the animal that so easily comes to mind. Around the turn of the last century, a badger game was a form of crime including prostitution, robbery, cons and extortion. It could include all four or any combination. The game also required more than one participant.

In its simplest terms, a badger game involved a man and a woman. The woman would pose as a reputable person who had fallen on hard times. She would approach a man, preferably married, who appeared honorable and wealthy. She would reluctantly propose to have a sexual encounter in exchange for money. Of course, she would impress upon him just how unusual such a request would be for her under normal circumstances.

Once the woman and her victim were alone, her accomplice would take one of many actions. He could sneak into the room while the lights were off and steal everything he could find of value among the victims' clothing. He could also storm into the room, acting like an outraged husband and threatening to fight the victim unless he parted with a specific amount of money. Another option was the crooks could threaten to inform the victim's family unless he paid them money to keep quiet.

In 1915, Ironton had its own version of the badger game. In this case, two women and one man were running the scam. Their antics would involve lawmen all over the tristate area.

The roots of this story begin on November 13, 1895, in Lawrence County, Ohio. On that date, Jacob W. Patterson was united in marriage to a woman named Susie. The couple eventually settled in a house at 615 Greenup Avenue in Ashland, Boyd County, Kentucky. In that house, they raised their five children. Jacob, often called J.W., worked at the local plat mill company as a hooker nail. Susie spent her days caring for her home, husband and children.

The Pattersons' older son, Richard, had strayed from the straight and narrow. His behavior would lead him to being arrested and spending time in the Catlettsburg, Kentucky jail.

While in jail, Richard met a man by the name of Charles Mullins. Born in Clay County, Kentucky, Charles had already lived a fairly difficult life. He had one alias, Charles Jones, but did not even know his actual age. Law enforcement estimated he was around twenty-two years old. He had been arrested and was serving time for larceny when he became friends with Richard.

When Charles was released from jail in Catlettsburg, Richard invited his new friend to stay at his family's home in Ashland. Richard's mother, Susie, found herself falling for the charm of her son's young friend. In July 1915, Susie would abandon her husband and four young children to be with her boyfriend.

Shortly after Susie left her family, her thirteen-year-old daughter, Nora, ran away from home. She had fallen in love with a twenty-one-year-old man from the 101 Ranch Wild West Show. She had run off to be with him.

The Wild West show stopped in Chillicothe, Ross County, Ohio, on September 11, 1913. The show performed two exhibitions in Chillicothe, one at 2:15 p.m. and the other at 8:15 p.m. Among the show's many attractions were hundreds of horses, scores of wagons and an Indian village. The allure of adventure on the road led Nora to leave her home and be with her love.

It wasn't long before Susie reunited with her daughter Nora. The mother and daughter began a crime spree with the assistance of Charles Mullins.

Jacob had tried to reunite his family to no avail. He appealed to his wife but gained no ground. Believing his wife had enticed his daughter to leave home, he tried to appeal to the local police to reunite him with Nora. The normal life he led held little appeal for his daughter.

Susie and Charles had found refuge in the home of Frances Smith. Frances was a well-known madam in Ironton's red-light district on Buckhorn Street. Once Nora joined her mother, Charles and Susie found housing elsewhere.

The threesome rented a room at an Ironton boardinghouse. Living off money from less-than-honest endeavors, they found themselves unable to

Chillicothe Gazette ad for Wild West show. Author's collection.

pay for their new home. The boardinghouse owner threw all three out onto the streets. Sadly, the owner forgot to collect his keys. Charles, Susie and Nora returned in the night and stole blankets, comforters and anything else they could find.

Their theft was uncovered when they tried to sell jewelry stolen from the boardinghouse. The local jewelry store became suspicious when they requested too little for some pieces and too much for others. The store employees, believing the items to be stolen, chose to refuse to purchase any items.

Lawrence County law enforcement was beginning to question Mullins's and the Pattersons' activities. Charles, Susie and Nora chose to leave Ironton before they were arrested.

Their next destination was Chillicothe, Ross County, Ohio. While in Chillicothe, the threesome began their own version of the badger game. Nora was assigned the job of luring men back to various locations. Once there, the hapless victim would be relieved of their valuables.

Nora led her victims to one of four locations. To escape the law and retribution from their victims, Charles, Susie and Nora moved regularly throughout the city. At first, they led their marks to a place on West Main Street. Their second residence was located on Mulberry Street between Fourth and Main Streets. Their home on East Fourth Street was next, and it would play a major role in their capture. Lastly, Mullins and the Pattersons lived on East Second Street. Sometimes Susie and Nora used a different place at night for their scam.

Nora was not just playing a role in the badger game. She was also playing with the heart of the son of a prominent man. Although he was not identified by name, the young man was relieved of various amounts of money over time. Nora referred to him only as her sweetheart. She claimed all she had to do was call him sweetheart to get her heart's desire.

Nora and Susie first aroused suspicion when they attempted to pawn more jewelry. They had in their possession two diamond rings. Susie claimed she had received one from a gentleman. The second ring was supposedly found by Nora while walking on the street.

The Mullins and Patterson scam ended on November 13, 1915. Mysterious gunshots were reported during the middle of the night. At first, the police had trouble figuring out who was firing the gun and to what purpose.

Then, a Norfolk and Western Railroad conductor saw Charles Mullins on the N&W bridge just south of the city. Mullins had pulled out a gun and threatened the man. He even went as far as to fire the gun in the man's direction before running away. The conductor reported what he had witnessed to the police. Officers George Hamm, Porter Haynes and Donald Swepsten arrived on scene to apprehend Mullins and two women on the north end of the bridge. The two women were later identified as Susie and Nora Patterson.

Charles had been caught red-handed with a revolver. He denied ever firing the weapon within the city limits, but that did not save him from being charged with carrying a concealed weapon.

The man who was Mullins's intended victim remained anonymous. All the newspaper would state was that the man was prominent in Chillicothe. His identity was concealed to protect his reputation and out of respect.

Once they were arrested, the gang began to tell their own tales. Susie claimed that Charles Jones, aka Charles Mullins, had been raised by her since he was a boy. Of course, she had met him only a few months before abandoning her family to be with him. Later she would refer to him as Charles Patterson. Finally, she admitted his name was Charles Mullins. One could not blame Susie—Charles even lost track of which name was actually his.

While Charles was being interviewed by the police, his tale was a bit different than Susie's. He adamantly denied being raised by Susie, but he did claim to have known her for a long time. He said he knew nothing about her husband or her remaining children. He denied ever having fired a gun within the Chillicothe city limits even though he had been caught red-handed with the evidence.

Charles's name was not the only thing confusing him. He seemed to have difficulty stating where he lived. Charles told the police he lived "in the state of Ohio." When that vague answer did not satisfy the authorities, he said he lived with Susie and Nora. Although this answer was nonspecific, it may have been the most accurate one he gave. The three had moved around so many times to escape the law and work their scams that an actual home base did not exist for them.

Born in Clay County, Kentucky, Charles even had trouble stating his age. He told the police he did not know his correct age but knew he had been raised in Clay County. The Chillicothe sheriff guessed his age to be twenty-two.

As for Nora, she claimed she was eighteen years old. Born on May 20, 1900, she was only fifteen years old.

Once their arrest became known, multiple people began to contact the Chillicothe police and the local newspapers. The Ashland, Kentucky police claimed Charles had run off with Susie. The police had arrested Mullins for larceny. He had spent time in the Catlettsburg jail. All of these troubles occurred before he and Susie paired up. They believed Nora had joined Susie later when she and Charles were in Ironton. When the Ironton police began searching for Nora to return her to her father and tried to arrest Mullins and Susie, the three sought a new place and new victims.

Susie's husband, Jacob Patterson, wrote a letter to the sheriff's office. He called Mullins a "thief, liar, bum." He requested Nora be placed in a reform school as punishment. For his wife and her lover, he asked that they be punished "as far as the law would let them go." Jacob said Susie had enticed Nora to run away from home. He hoped Susie would face white slavery charges for her actions.

Lastly, the Ironton police chimed in. They admitted they had been trying to capture Charles and Susie. At the time, they were just hoping to return Nora to her father. They had some trouble determining if Nora had been living in a local house of "ill fame" or whorehouse. According to Susie, she and Charles had moved out of the whorehouse before Nora joined them.

After all the evidence was gathered, Charles was charged with carrying a concealed weapon in Chillicothe, Ohio. He was arraigned in the mayor's court on November 15, 1915. He was bound over to a grand jury. His bail was set at $500. Eventually, Charles pleaded guilty. His story seems to end there.

Susie was also charged. Unlike Charles, she was charged with loitering. She was found guilty. The local judge gave her a choice: leave Chillicothe by sundown on November 30, 1915, or be incarcerated in the Xenia workhouse and pay a fifty-dollar fine. Since Susie did not have any money, she could not take a train back to Ironton. When asked what she was going to do, Susie told reporters she would gladly walk the ninety miles back to Ironton rather than remain in Chillicothe.

Before they parted, Susie requested Nora be released. Rather than be returned to her father, Susie suggested custody of Nora be given to her aunt who lived in Ironton. By December 1915, no action had been taken on Susie's suggestion.

Susie did leave Chillicothe on time. She was able to remain free. She may have returned to Jacob, but one would doubt that. By 1930, she had remarried.

Nora returned to a normal-ish life after her life of crime. She married in 1924, and she and her husband settled down in Lawrence County, Ohio.

12

BOWMAN VERSUS STAPLETON

*M*ary Jane and Jane Smith were sisters. Both were born in Ohio, and Mary Jane was the older of the two, being born around 1854. Jane was born less than six years later.

Mary Jane was the first to marry. She and her husband, Milton Bowman, would have five children together.

Jane was not as lucky as her older sister. It appears that she married more than once. Although marriage records have not been located for these early marriages, she had two children listed as sons in the 1880 census. The oldest was Robert King (born around 1872), followed by James Walters (born around 1876). If these two children were born during two separate marriages, Jane was definitely unlucky in love.

On January 3, 1880, Jane said "I do" one more time. This time she chose Joseph Stapleton as her husband.

The Bowman and Stapleton families were close by choice or forced by life. Both families lived in the same house on Etna Street near Seventh Street in Ironton, Ohio.

Although close in proximity, the two men possessed dramatically different personalities. Milton was known as a peaceful man.

Joseph was well known by the police. He had served time on the chain gang just before his marriage to Jane.

Despite their differences, both Milton and Joseph were having trouble finding jobs to support their growing families. The two men were forced to take any odd jobs or chores they could find.

Unlike many women of the period, Mary and Jane worked outside of their homes. Both found jobs as dishwashers at the same Ironton hotel. These jobs not only brought in much-needed income but also gave them the ability to bring home food. Scraps and leftovers from the hotel's guests helped feed the two households.

The Stapleton household consisted of Joseph, Jane, eight-year-old Robert King and four-year-old James Walters.

The Bowman household consisted of Milton, Mary and their children: nine-year-old E.R., five-year-old John W. and two one-year-old twins, Mary and Mattie. On February 24, 1880, Mary delivered their fifth child, a girl named Girtie Lillie Bowman.

Both families were struggling. Work for the men was hard to come by. The women worked hard at the hotel only to come home to face endless chores as mothers and wives. Such desperate times can lead to desperate acts.

One April evening in 1880, the hard times took a violent turn. Mary and Jane had returned from work with their meager offerings from the hotel's tables. After work, they met in Jane's home. The sisters were dividing the scraps they had brought home when they began to argue. Things continued to heat up as Jane and Mary quarreled. As the argument escalated, harsh words were exchanged.

Palace Hotel, one of the first hotels in Ironton. *Author's collection.*

What began as a minor disagreement soon morphed into a physical altercation. At one point, Jane grabbed her older sister by her hair and started to force her out of the house.

With Mary no longer in the house, Milton began to argue with Jane. He was determined to get his family's fair share of the scraps his wife had brought home. Eventually, Jane's husband, Joseph, could stand no more. He entered the fray and demanded Milton leave.

Milton informed his in-laws he would gladly leave just as soon as he found a home to house his family.

Milton's answer not only did not satisfy his in-laws, but it also seemed to inflame Joseph. Joseph knocked Milton to the ground and began to pummel him.

The arguing and fighting caught the attention of the neighbors. They were surprised to see Stapleton on top of Bowman, striking him over and over again. Jane tried to catch her husband's arm to prevent him from injuring Milton further.

Not content with using his fists, Joseph reached for a weapon. His hands found a hot flatiron used to iron clothes. Much like a modern iron in shape, flatirons were much heavier and heated by placing them on a stove.

Joseph used the iron to mash and burn Milton on his head and face, but that was not enough. Joseph then used a knife to strike fatal blows on the unconscious Milton Bowman.

A neighbor, Sarah Johnson, was one of the witnesses to the attack. A woman of color, she overcame any misgivings about how her statement might be perceived and told the police what she saw. She stated Joseph did not act alone. Jane had also participated in the attack. She had used the same flatiron as her husband to strike her brother-in-law.

As Milton lay in a pool of his own blood, Joseph realized he was being watched. He dropped his weapons and fled across the Ohio River into Kentucky. He escaped to the Siegert's Creek area.

When help finally arrived, they found Milton lying on his dirty bed groaning and breathing hard. A reporter was allowed in to see Milton even though he was not conscious. The reporter saw the many blows from which Milton was suffering. One of the worst blows from the hot iron landed on his right cheek. A slash from a knife marred his forehead, while another ghastly wound was found on the back of his head.

At first, the doctors thought Milton might survive the assault, but he was not so lucky. Milton Bowman died on April 5, 1880, at 10:00 p.m.

Old Lawrence County Courthouse in Ironton. *Briggs Lawrence County Public Library, Hamner Room.*

The postmortem on the deceased gave evidence to the brutality of the attack. His skull had been broken. His brain had been compressed by the numerous ruptured blood vessels.

With Joseph hiding in Kentucky, Jane alone faced the police. She was taken into custody that evening. Jane Stapleton spent four days in the Lawrence County, Ohio jail before being acquitted.

As for Joseph Stapleton, his name never appeared in the Lawrence County, Ohio jail register, nor did he serve time in the Ohio State Penitentiary for his crime.

The 1880 Federal Census provides some information about the two families. Milton was not listed in the Bowman household, and Mary was listed as a widow. Her youngest child, born just months before the vicious attack, was not listed. This absence may have indicated the child had passed or was just ignored by the census taker.

As for the Stapletons, Joseph was listed as the head of the household. The census did state he had been unemployed for four months during the previous year. Had he returned to his family? It is possible but not guaranteed. Census takers often recorded household members regardless of whether they were present or not.

After the 1880 census, the Bowmans and Stapletons seem to disappear. No one from the households appears in any local record. Even Milton's final resting place was not recorded.

Their tale lives on only in newspaper articles written at the time of the attack.

13

FEMME FATALE

The Story of Nancy Patterson Moreland

*N*ancy "Nan" Patterson was known as the belle of the hills. Born on November 26, 1902, in a log cabin in Kitts Hill, Lawrence County, Ohio, she was one of ten children. Her parents were John and Sarah Wise Patterson.

Like her siblings, Nan attended the local rural schools. Even then, her striking beauty caught the attention of the opposite sex. Many of her male classmates wrote her love notes.

At the tender age of sixteen, Nan left home for a different life. She thought she would find it in the city of Ironton.

When World War I broke out, she did her patriotic duty. She began working in a local factory. This job provided her the ability to explore her fashion sense. She was able to buy her first fancy dresses, shoes and silk stockings. The little country girl was growing up.

As she aged, Nan's beauty did not diminish. She was often surrounded by suitors of all ages and sizes.

Nan was described as a dark-haired beauty with a caressing voice. She had a lovely complexion and a voluptuous figure.

Her beauty, however, could not compare to her personality. Her outer beauty may have caught men's eyes, but her personality caused them to fall in love.

At the age of eighteen, Nan Patterson chose to say yes to one of her many suitors. Charles Bentley was the lucky man. They were united in wedlock on August 28, 1920, in Lawrence County, Ohio. Charles worked for the railroad. Nan and Charles were well liked and had numerous friends. During her marriage to Charles, Nan became known as an excellent cook.

The honeymoon phase of their marriage did not last long. Nan and Charles divorced.

Once single, Nan was surrounded by suitors. Two men rose to the top: Herman Moreland and Howard Bartram.

Born on January 1, 1893, in Ironton, Ohio, Herman Moreland was nearly ten years older than Nan. The son of Andrew and Mary Huckingburger Moreland, Herman had already been married before. Some reports say he was a widower, but his first wife, Rose Zornes, did not die until 1939. He and Rose had at least three daughters: Helen Lucille, Mary Catherine and Nell Rose.

Her second suitor was Howard Bartram. Known as Bubbles to his friends and family, he worked with his brother Norman at his meat market on South Seventh Street in Ironton. Only a few months separated Howard and Nan's age. He was one of six children born to Louis and Mary Bartram.

In the end, Herman was the one who won Nan's heart. They were married around 1926.

Howard was not happy with Nan's choice. He was not willing to give up, even though she had married another.

Several months after Nan and Herman married, Howard and Herman argued. According to the rumors, Howard had been bragging that Nan loved him more than her new husband. This meeting was the first of many quarrels between the two men. All of the arguments were over Nan. It had been nearly

Kitts Hill High School. *Author's collection.*

two years since Herman and Nan were married, but the identity of the man who truly held her heart was still under contention. It was not long before the animosity between her husband and her former suitor led to a physical attack.

Once again, Herman and Howard argued. Howard held a grudge and was not letting their troubles end.

On Wednesday, January 11, 1928, Howard Bartram was overheard threatening Herman. Howard had planned to get his brother Stanley and "get Moreland."

Often called Si, Stanley Bartram was not like his brother. At thirty-two, he was already married to Mary Conway. He and Mary had

Nancy "Nan" Patterson Moreland. *Author's collection.*

a three-year-old daughter, Rosemary. He worked with his brother John. He may have accompanied his brother Howard in an attempt to be a peacemaker. With his presence, Si was hoping to end the quarrel and stop any violence.

While Howard was recruiting Si to his older brother to aid in his conflict with Herman, Moreland had already heard of the threat. He went to the Ironton police looking to prevent further conflict. Even though he reported the threat, Herman found himself facing the Bartram brothers alone.

The three men—Herman Moreland, Howard Bartram and Stanley Bartram—met face-to-face on Thursday, January 12, around six o'clock in the evening. They met at the rear entrance of Davies Store near the corner of Second and Lawrence Streets in Ironton. Since the meeting occurred behind the store, the three men escaped the notice of the public for a while.

Since there was a lack of independent witnesses to the beginning of the attack, there are more guesses about what happened than actual facts. The Bartram brothers and Moreland did enter into a physical fight. Howard did strike Herman multiple times.

Si made multiple attempts to stop the fight. Sadly, he was unsuccessful.

Things escalated quickly when Herman Moreland pulled a .32 Iver-Johnson hammering revolver from his coat and fired two shots. His first shot struck Si.

"He got me," cried Si as he fell to the ground.

Howard and Herman continued to trade punches. Herman's gun failed to fire again, so he was forced to use it as a club. He struck Howard Bartram over his right eye.

D.C. Davies Dry Goods Store. *Author's collection.*

The gunshots finally caught the attention of everyone nearby. Constable John Crance had been stationed on the northwest corner of Third and Lawrence. He did not see the beginning of the conflict, but he rushed to the scene when he heard the shots fired. He arrived in time to see Herman strike Howard with the gun and Stanley fall to the ground.

When Herman saw Crance, he offered no resistance. He handed the constable his gun. Crance placed him under arrest.

Harry Slaughter of Mill Street and Tom Norris of Park Avenue were as close as Constable Crance. Like Crance, they did not see what began the argument. Slaughter, however, offered assistance in placing Stanley in a car.

Both Bartram brothers were taken to the Marting Hospital on Fifth Street. Stanley was examined at the hospital, and the doctors noticed the bullet had entered his abdomen. It had entered his left side, puncturing his large intestine before burying itself in the fleshy part of his left hip. He had severe internal hemorrhages and was in critical condition. Dr. William F. Marting, owner and founder of the hospital, operated on Stanley.

When Howard was released from the hospital, he went to his home at 916 North Fifth Street in Ironton. He did not plan on resting and relaxing. He wanted revenge. He picked up his revolver and hid it beneath his sweater. His next destination was the county jail.

When Howard arrived at the Ironton jail, he asked the desk sergeant to see Moreland. Stewart, the desk sergeant, informed Howard he would have to be searched before seeing Moreland.

Before Stewart could search him, Howard pulled his revolver from beneath his sweater. He shoved the gun against Chief Dennis Callahan, who had been walking by. Callahan swept the gun away and charged at Howard.

Art Jones, a brother to Mayor Harry Jones, was at the jail. When he saw Howard and Callahan struggling, he stepped in to help the police. Art grabbed the gun's barrel.

With Art, Callahan and Howard struggling over control of the gun, minutes flew by. No one was giving up easily. Then, the revolver's trigger was pulled accidently. Thankfully, Art still had a firm grasp on the barrel. He had been aiming the gun toward the floor just in case it fired. The bullet ripped through the floor.

After the gun discharged, Callahan was able to wrestle free from Howard. He freed his own gun from the holster. This task was made even more difficult because his wrist had been injured in the fight.

Once faced with Callahan's gun, Howard surrendered. He was taken to the county jail to keep him separate from Herman.

On January 12, 1928, Howard Bartram was arraigned before Justice P.A. Burke. He was charged with shooting with the intent to kill and carrying a concealed weapon.

Moreland was arraigned by the same justice on the same day. He, too, was charged with shooting with the intent to kill. Reporters from the *Ironton Tribune* attempted to interview him at the jail, but he refused to discuss his case in any way.

On January 13, Stanley's condition was stated as serious. His brother and his attacker were freed on a $1,000 bond.

On January 15, Herman Moreland's preliminary hearing was postponed. Stanley's condition was still way too uncertain. The court did not want to proceed until Stanley Bartram's condition was finally known.

The court and Herman had to wait sixteen days before a conclusion was reached. Tragically for the Bartram family, the conclusion was Stanley's death.

WICKED LAWRENCE COUNTY, OHIO

Stanley had been taken to his parents' home a week before he died. In the end, the bullet did not kill, but it did contribute to his death. While recovering from the shooting, he developed pneumonia. In his weakened condition, he was unable to fight off the infection. He died peacefully at 7:45 a.m. on January 31, 1928.

Undertakers Gholson and Sons were called in to assist with the body. Stanley "Si" Bartram's funeral was held at his parents' home on February 3, 1928, at 2:00 p.m. He was laid to rest in Woodland Cemetery, Ironton, Ohio.

When Herman finally faced the grand jury, he was looking at murder charges. After hearing all the evidence from eyewitnesses, the grand jury refused to charge Herman with any crime. They believed the shooting was a result of a fight. Herman had been defending himself against Howard and Stanley.

Howard Bartram was not satisfied with the jury's findings. He had seen Herman as an enemy before. Now, he really had a reason to hate Moreland. He would wait years to finally get his revenge.

As for Herman, he may have been found not guilty, but the community was not so certain. He had trouble finding steady work.

In order to support their family, Nan and Herman decided to take advantage of Nan's admired cooking skills. They opened Nan's Sandwich Shoppe on the second floor of New System Baking Company. The restaurant specialized in chicken and spaghetti dinners. For those who were looking for more liquid refreshment, a couple gallons of moonshine was kept hidden in the kitchen.

After the shooting, Howard continued to work for his brother John. In July 1933, he had a day off from work. He used a physician's prescription to purchase some drugstore whiskey. Prohibition was the rule of the land. The only way to purchase alcohol legally was with a doctor's prescription. This alcohol became known as drugstore whiskey because the only place to purchase it was at a pharmacy.

Then, Howard Bartram walked into the Eagles Hall on the corner of Third and Railroad Streets in Ironton. He found a comfortable chair and dozed through the afternoon.

Unaware of Howard's presence, Herman Moreland walked into the Eagles. He joined G.W. "Wash" Payne in a game of pool.

When Payne left, Moreland walked into the card room to play rummy. Charles Warton, Charles Harker, Edward Gallagher, Ed Gavin and Elmer Costello were already in the room. They joined Moreland in a card game.

Willard "Beefsteak" Staten had been asked to join the group playing rummy, but he declined and left the room. Carl Harbolt and Robert Powers were also in the room but were content to just watch the game.

When Herman left the poolroom, Howard awoke from his slumber. He made his way to the club's bar and ordered a drink. He was later joined by Staten.

After Howard finished his drink, he left the Eagles in his automobile parked outside. He was gone for only a short time before returning to the clubhouse.

"Bud" Williams spotted Howard upon his return. He saw Howard fumbling with something as he walked toward the card room.

Robert Powers had positioned himself just inside the doorway as he watched the card game unfold. Howard pushed him from the doorway.

Once in the card room, he leveled the gun at Herman Moreland. He told Moreland, "Now you big —— say something."

Moreland attempted to rise from his chair to face Howard. He began to plead with Bartram not to shoot him. His pleading did nothing to deter Howard.

Carl Harbolt made an attempt to stop Howard. He grabbed his gun wrist, but Howard shook him off.

Howard did not even give Herman the chance to stand before he shot him. The first shot struck Herman high in the right side of his chest. The bullet ripped through his body before emerging from the left side of his back.

With the first shot, the card players scattered. Edward "Candy" Gallagher was sitting next to Herman when the first shot was fired. He quickly exited his chair. Just after he moved from his chair, a shot struck one rung of his chair, missing him by inches. After it hit the chair, the bullet went through the door leading into the lodge's poolroom.

A second shot struck Herman three inches below his right nipple. It emerged from the center of his back. These two bullet strikes caused Herman to lurch forward. He was dying before the second shot even left the gun.

Everyone had fled from the room. Howard was left alone with his victim as Herman lay dying.

Andy Kady, the lodge's custodian, and Willard "Beefsteak" Staten were in the lodge's lunchroom. The lunchroom was next door to the card room.

Howard left the card room after his second shot found a home in Herman's body. He walked into the lunch room next door. He calmly ordered a glass of beer. Then, he made his way back to the card room. As he stood over Herman's body, he said, "You big —— you should have gotten this years ago."

With those final words, Howard fired the last bullet in his gun. It struck Herman in his neck.

Kady told Bartram that he should have not killed Herman. Bartram's response was to point his gun at Kady. He warned him not to say anything. Howard handed his gun to Kady so he could give it to the police.

With his warning to Kady, Howard calmly walked out of the lodge. He walked over to his car, which was parked in front of Schachletter's Cafe. Howard then drove to his mother's home.

At his parents' home, Howard told his mother he had shot and killed Herman Moreland. He gathered some money left in the house and went back to his car.

Howard's next move was to drive down Fifth Street in Ironton toward the river highway or what we refer to as Old 52. First, he headed to Portsmouth in Scioto County, Ohio. Then he doubled back, hoping to confuse the police and avoid capture.

One of the bystanders called Nan. She hurried to the lodge and arrived in time to witness Herman's last breath.

Herman Moreland's funeral was held at the O'Keefe Funeral Home. He was buried in Woodland Cemetery in Ironton, Ohio. He left behind three daughters—Lucille, Mary Catherine and Nell Rose—as well as Nan.

The search for Howard Bartram continued. Nan had sworn out a warrant for his arrest for the murder of Herman in the court of Squire F.B. Davies.

Howard drove back and forth across Lawrence and Scioto Counties to escape the police. On July 26, 1933, he was spotted at Pine Grove. He had cut cross-country from Powellsville and South Webster to avoid the Scioto County and Jackson County sheriffs. Witnesses said he was driving a Willys-Knight coupe.

The next day, first-degree murder charges were filed against Howard Bartram by the state. An inquest was scheduled for July 28 at 10:00 a.m. in the courthouse. Coroner Harry Jones presided over the inquest. Howard, however, was still at large.

After Howard left Pine Grove, he drove toward Jackson, Jackson County, Ohio. He visited a former Irontonian named Pete Dobbins. Dobbins owned a restaurant in Jackson, and Howard stopped by to buy a sandwich.

After his meal at Dobbins's place, he drove to Chillicothe, Ohio. He still had no plans to surrender. He traveled to Columbus and Fostoria, Ohio, before returning to Ironton.

On July 28, as the inquest was being held, Howard surrendered to Sheriff Ernest Bennett, Lawrence County's sheriff, at 4:00 p.m. Three days later, he

Willys-Knight coupe. *Author's collection.*

stood before Magistrate Fred B. Davies. Prosecuting attorney John Porter was chosen to represent the state. Judge E.E. Corn and attorney J.W. Byrne were hired to represent the defense.

Shockingly, he was given a bond of $7,000. His brother Norman Bartram, Harold Fetters and Charles Smith pooled their resources to pay the bond. Howard Bartram was freed.

Nan continued to operate Nan's Sandwich Shoppe. Her place had become popular with local politicians and public officials at lunchtime. In the evenings, the place was frequented by younger men. Many claimed the restaurant's success had more to do with the owner's beauty than with the food and illegal booze. They said she had a way of making men believe she had feelings for them without actually following through with the expected actions. Eventually, Nan was able to obtain a legal beer license after selling illegal beer for years.

With Herman's death, Nan found herself once again inundated with suitors. One of her most ardent admirers was prosecuting attorney John Porter. Even though she had a string of admirers, Nan was a respectable woman. She also was quite smart and a savvy businesswoman.

John Porter was thirty-five years old. A World War I veteran, he had been exposed to poisonous gasses. Poisonous gas was a whole new type of warfare created by the Germans. John's exposure led to his being hospitalized in France. Even after he returned from Europe, John suffered from shell shock and anxiety.

Shell shock has come to be known as post-traumatic stress disorder. At that time in history, little was known about the condition or how to treat it.

In John's case, his nervous condition even resulted in him refusing to drive a car. He claimed he was too anxious to drive safely.

John had not always been a lawyer. He had been a brakeman on the Chesapeake and Ohio Railroad for a while. He studied law at night with the help of an Ironton law office. Once he completed his studies, it took John two times before he passed the Ohio State Bar.

In his personal life, John Porter married Lillian Whiteman in Canada. They had two children, James and Bruce.

Porter passed the bar in 1931. He ran for the Lawrence County prosecutor office in 1932. He truly did not believe he had a chance to win. He was wrong. John Porter was elected as the county prosecutor on his first try.

One of his first cases was the case against Howard Bartram. He became a frequent visitor at Nan's Sandwich Shoppe. Then, he became an admirer of hers.

On October 25, 1933, John and Nan went for a drive into the country. They had been seen by witnesses earlier in the evening at a speakeasy. Supposedly, they were quarreling about another man paying Nan attention. After their trip to the country, John took Nan back to her home above the restaurant.

The next day, John returned to Nan's shop. Some people claimed he had been unruly. His behavior became so bad Nan threatened to hit him with a bottle if he disturbed her business anymore.

Porter left the restaurant after a while. He returned a little later after purchasing a banjo and a pistol.

Purchasing the gun had been no easy task. John did not want to purchase the gun himself. Instead, he went to a friend, Lou Smith. He told Lou he wanted a "gat." At first, Lou thought he wanted a blackjack, a baton-like weapon, but John quickly corrected him.

Lou went to Central Hardware at 110 South Second Street in Ironton. There he purchased a .32-caliber Harrington and Richardson revolver for nine dollars.

Porter gave Lou a check for sixteen dollars: five dollars for the banjo and nine for the gun. Two dollars remained from the check, but what those two dollars purchased was not recorded. Perhaps it was a bonus given to Lou for his help. The two men parted ways around 3:30 p.m. Then, John returned to Nan's.

He and Nan went into her room above the restaurant. Their time alone was far from peaceful. They were interrupted by a police raid.

Sheriff Ernest W. Bennett received an anonymous call. The caller suggested the sheriff raid Nan's flat for illegal whiskey. When the police arrived, they found John and Nan scantily clad and drunk.

Downtown Ironton with Central Hardware. *Briggs Lawrence County Public Library, Hamner Room.*

The sheriff chose not to arrest anyone. He assumed the call had been politically motivated. One of Porter's enemies was trying to tarnish his reputation. In the end, they did not raid the apartment or restaurant. All they did was tell Porter to go home.

Unfortunately for everyone involved, Nan did not send Porter home. It would be a fatal mistake.

Sometime later, a shot rang out. All the apartment's doors and windows were locked and bolted. Rescuers were forced to break in. Gilbert Flowers, a cook at Nan's Sandwich Shoppe, pried open the doors to Nan's apartment. Several of the male customers helped him gain access to the apartment. They were not prepared for what they saw.

Nan was lying on the floor on one side of the bed. She was wearing silk pajamas but was described as scantily clad. She had powder burns on her shoulder. The large amount of blood on her side of the bed led officers to speculate that she had been on the bed when shot. A spent bullet was found beneath her stomach.

John Porter lay on the bed face-down. He was on the opposite side from Nan. Porter was wearing only his underclothes. Blood spatters on his side of the bed indicated he had not been lying down when he was shot.

The gun lay on Nan's side of the floor.

Identified as a guitar in some accounts, the banjo was found on the floor at the foot of the bed.

Both Nan and John were unconscious. Bingaman and Jones's ambulance was called in to transfer them to the Marting Hospital. John was in serious condition when he arrived at the hospital. A bullet had entered under his right eye and exited above his left eye.

Nan had been shot in front of her right ear. Instead of exiting, the bullet lodged in her forehead above her left eye. She never regained consciousness and died at 5:10 p.m., two hours after the shooting.

A postmortem was performed on Nan at the Deaconess Hospital by Dr. C.E. Vidt and Dr. William F. Marting. Dr. Cooper from Ashland, Kentucky, was brought in to examine the X-rays.

Nan's remains were taken to O'Keefe Funeral Home. Reverend W.H. Hamptom officiated. Like her late husband, Nan was buried in Woodland Cemetery.

On October 29, John Porter regained consciousness. He had lost his left eye, but he was able to see out of his right eye. His wife, Lillian, was by his side the entire time he was in the hospital.

On October 30, the police were still trying to determine what happened. It appeared to be a murder-suicide situation, but who was the victim? Who was the killer?

One person at the scene overheard a police officer say, "Nan, why did you do it?"

Flowers claimed the shooting may have been caused by jealousy. Nan had gone on a date with a schoolteacher from one of the rural schools on Friday. John and Nan quarreled on Saturday morning after Nan returned home. Flowers stated there were numerous customers in the restaurant, but he was unable to say who they were.

Another witness, Ernestine Francis, was Nan's niece. She was questioned like Flowers, but could testify only about what she heard.

No one had been in the apartment when the actual shooting took place except Nan and John.

John Porter's friends had a completely different view of the events and his relationship to Nan. They claimed Porter was there only on business. He was interviewing Nan about Herman's shooting.

The doctors refused to allow John to be questioned until November 10. When he was able to speak, John Porter blamed Nan. He had been told by people he should stay away from Nan, but he did not listen. On that fateful day when he returned to Nan's place, he claimed, she was so drunk she could barely stand. He helped her to her bedroom, so she could lie down. She pulled the gun as they argued, and he was trying to disarm Nan when the gun accidentally went off.

On November 8, 1933, an inquest was to be held. One problem arose when the state did not have anyone to represent it. The inquest had to be delayed until a temporary prosecutor could be appointed.

With so many questions left unanswered, John Porter could not be expected to return to his job as prosecutor. Judge Dan C. Jones appointed Wayne L. Elkins of South Point to replace Porter. Elkins had a reputation for fighting illicit liquor sales, which had been rampant in the county for years.

After the shooting, John began exhibiting strange behavior. He lost control of himself. At times, he had violent outbursts. In and out of court, he made incoherent arguments and statements. Not only was he irrational, but he also had an inexplicable dislike of his old friends.

At the same time, Coroner Harry J. Jones held John Porter responsible for the shooting. He recommended charges be brought against Porter.

Attorney H.A. McGowan was chosen to represent Nan's family.

On November 10, 1933, John Porter was officially charged with first-degree murder. He was arraigned before Fred Davies, justice of the peace. Porter pleaded not guilty and was held on a $5,000 bond.

As his mental state continued to decline, John found himself unable to return to his job. He officially resigned as a prosecutor on November 27, 1933. On December 5, 1933, Wayne Elkins permanently replaced Porter as the Lawrence County prosecutor.

On January 25, 1934, Porter faced the grand jury. He was considered fully recovered from his injuries and about to find out what his future would be. The jury found there was just not enough evidence for a conviction. With Nan dead and the only witness being John, they felt the case would not end in a guilty verdict.

John Porter had requested to be removed from the Ohio State Bar. His request was granted. However, when he was exonerated, he attempted to be readmitted. He was not.

Howard Bartram had been awaiting trial for his killing of Herman Moreland through all the ups and downs in Porter's case. Even though there were many witnesses and the case had appeared to be open and shut, Howard was acquitted after a jury trial.

14

MURDER ON TICK RIDGE

Friendship means many things for different people. In Lawrence County, Ohio, friends are often fiercely protective of each other and their link to each other. Trying to cause problems among friends can bring about many results, up to and including death.

On March 19, 1956, at 1:00 a.m., two brothers' lives would end while trying to protect their bond and punish the person trying to destroy their friendship with another Lawrence Countian.

James and Herbert Hoover Large were separated by six years. James was born on October 14, 1924, in Greenup, Greenup County, Kentucky. Called Hoover by friends and family, Herbert was born in Lawrence County, Ohio, on August 21, 1930. Both were sons of Lewis and Delia Matthews Large.

James had moved around trying to find a permanent place. He had lived near Chesapeake, Ohio; in Akron, Ohio; and in Greenup County, Ohio.

Hoover seemed to spend most of his time in Lawrence County, Ohio.

By 1956, both brothers had moved to Lawrence County to live with their sister Mae Mullins. Mae had married C.H. Mullins and lived on Greenville Hill near Waterloo, Ohio.

While living with their sister, they became acquainted with a Lawrence Countian named David Daniels. Daniels had a small four-room house on Tick Ridge. Consisting of two bedsteads, a table and a cabinet, the Daniels home was a typical bachelor house.

James and Hoover became friends with David. They even started staying at his home for days at a time. The allure of the Daniels house may have been the amount of illegal moonshine that could be found there.

Tick Ridge. *Author's collection.*

Regardless of why they were friends, they were friends. For months, they spent days together. When night fell, the brothers would often sleep on the mattresses covered with blankets that Daniels called beds.

At 1:35 a.m. on March 19, 1956, David Daniels made a call to the sheriff's office. He simply stated he had killed the two Large brothers. Deputies John Drake, Elmer Carrico and Dean Dillon were the first on the scene.

The deputies found the two dead bodies of the Large brothers. James, aged thirty-two, lay near the house's fireplace. Hoover was stretched out on a mass of old rags covering an old mattress on the floor, one of David's so-called beds.

Lying close to one of the bloody corpses was Elbert Daniels. The cousin of David Daniels, he was the only witness to the events leading up to the shootings. His sleeping form lying on blood-soaked rags exhibited either severe intoxication or complete disregard for the events of the morning. The former was most likely.

Sheriff Carl Ross took David's statement. David had been fast asleep when he was rudely awakened by pounding on his door. It was the Large brothers. Being familiar with the men and seeing them as friends, he let them in.

According to Daniels, the Larges immediately began attacking David and Elbert. James squared off with David while Hoover struck Elbert over and over again. To defend himself, David began shooting James. He claimed he continued to fire at him until James let him go.

Once James fell to the floor, David turned his attention to Hoover. A single shot was all it took to stop Hoover's attack on David's cousin.

Realizing he needed to contact the law right away, David set off to find a phone. He went to the home of his sister-in-law, Della Daniels, to use her landline. Della was the one to call and inform the sheriff's office of the shooting.

When asked what may have caused the attack, David claimed the Larges were clear on their reason. They had been friends with not just David Daniels but also his brother. They claimed David had been deliberately causing conflict between them and David's brother.

As the sheriff and his deputies examined the crime scene, they began to question David's account of the event. The physical evidence just did not match with David's version. Their preliminary investigation caused them to question his account even more.

Elbert was little help to investigators. He claimed he had been drunk when he finally found his way to bed around ten o'clock the previous evening. He did not recall anyone striking him. According to Elbert, he remained asleep until he felt someone falling on him. That person was no doubt Hoover Large. Although Elbert had a small cut across his forehead, he had no other bruises or injuries typical of an assault.

It seems Elbert was not the only one to have been intoxicated. David also admitted he had been drinking heavily before going to bed on March 18.

James Large lay near the fireplace. According to David, James had fallen with his head in the fireplace. David had moved his body so it was farther away from the fireplace.

James's body had been shot three times. One entrance wound was in the middle of his lower chest and angled down. Two shots were to his head. One bullet had entered the middle of his forehead and came out the top of his head. The second head shot had entered his right temple and exited his left temple. Either one could have been the fatal shot.

Hoover had been shot only once by David. A single shot to the head ended his life at the age of twenty-five. The bullet had struck him on the left side of his nose. There were no exit wounds.

Neither body showed any evidence of the fight. Their hands and knuckles were free of any bruises or cuts. If they had been in a fistfight before their deaths as David claimed, their hands would have provided proof.

Coroner Dr. Harry Nenni was summoned to conduct the autopsy. He confirmed James and Hoover had both died from gunshot wounds to the head.

Hoover and James's bodies were taken to Phillips Funeral Home at six o'clock on the morning of the shooting. Reverend Walter Adams officiated the double funeral. The brothers were buried in Hecla Cemetery.

Hecla Cemetery. *Author's collection.*

The deputies also found a moonshine still thirty yards below David's house. The one-barrel still was located in a ravine and may have been linked to the shooting. No doubt liquor from the still provided the method for David and Elbert to be intoxicated on May 18 and 19. It may have also brought the Large brothers to David's home multiple times. A path was found that led directly from the house to the still. Both David and Elbert, however, claimed no knowledge of the nearby still. Since the still was obviously illegal, it was destroyed by the police.

Sheriff Ross called upon the Bureau of Identification and Investigation from London, Ohio, to help investigate the case. Criminologist Joe Martini headed that portion of the case. The bureau took blood samples and took the official photographs of the scene. They also conducted ballistic tests and a paraffin test on David. The paraffin test showed David had fired a gun recently. Of course, that fact had already been admitted by David.

The gun itself had a strange tale. It was a .32-caliber automatic pistol. David had purchased the gun just a week before the shooting. What had prompted David to make such a purchase? Did the timing mean anything special?

To help prove his version of the events was true, David Daniels agreed to take a lie detector test. He traveled to Columbus, Ohio, where the test was performed. Instead of proving him truthful, David's lie detector proved just the opposite. He had failed the test. Luckily for him, the lie detector test was inadmissible in court.

When questioned about his account's truthfulness, David said, "Well, I'll tell you the truth, I'm not sorry I shot them. I'm just sorry I had to do it."

Prosecutor Harold Spears was assigned to take the case to court. E.L. Riley and W.J. Curry represented the defense. Judge Warren S. Earhart was to oversee the trial.

A jury of eight women and four men was impaneled: Blanche H. Edelson, Helen C. Kleinman, Bealah Mays, Mae Primm, Dorothy Scherer, Lottie M. Banks, Lois McKnight, Ann Elizabeth Hacker, Leo O. Mulligan, Carl William Reed, Hugh Gibson and Mart Shaffer. One of their many duties was to tour the crime scene.

Forty-two witnesses were called to take the stand. Sheriff Deputy Elmer Carrico had been to the Daniels home early. He testified that David appeared to be completely unbothered about killing two people.

Joe Martini took the stand to state the results of his part of the investigation. One of the tests he performed required him to fire the gun used by David in the shooting. He stated the gun was defective and forced the user to operate the gun manually. The gun would also jam on every other shot.

The gun's defective condition affected how James was shot. Since James had been shot six times, including the three that struck his body, the shots could not have been quickly delivered. Plus, the shotgun was twelve to twenty-four inches from James at one time. The shot to his right temple was delivered while the gun was two and a half feet away.

As for Hoover, he had been shot only once. The shot that killed him had come when David was standing two to two and a half foot away.

Elbert Daniels took the stand as well. He was no more helpful during the court proceedings than in the investigation. He claimed he had no knowledge of the fight before the shooting. He also denied knowing about the still so close to David's home.

When David spoke, he stated he had never had any trouble before with James and Hoover Large. However, that night, James Large had said they were going to kill him. In fact, James said he was going to kill him the night David shot him. David admitted James's comments had made him angry, but his killing the two Large brothers was self-defense.

After everyone had testified, the jury deliberated for four and a half hours before reaching a verdict. They found David guilty of two counts of second-degree murder.

15

THE BELLE IN THE WELL

*U*nsolved mysteries can be found in every town, burg and city across the country. Some sit gathering dust in the basements of courthouses and police stations. Some cases capture the minds of the populace and law enforcement and never let go.

The Belle in the Well was one of those cases in Lawrence County, Ohio. Thankfully, her case was solved, but her story still haunts the county.

Her story starts in a rural part of Lawrence County, Ohio. Near Dobbston, two sisters, Tammy and Cathy Baxter, made a gruesome discovery in a covered cistern on April 21, 1981. They rushed home to get their father. He would know how to handle such a discovery.

The cistern was located on an abandoned property where the skeletal remains of a burned house stood. Locals knew the house had burned around 1973, but the actual date was not remembered at the time. The cistern had been covered with blocks and wood beams to keep animals and people from falling in it.

Since the property had been abandoned, it had become a hangout location for various groups. The site's most common visitors were biker groups.

Local law enforcement and fire departments quickly arrived on the scene. They drained the cistern to make recovering the body much easier.

Once the body had been rescued from the cistern, the investigation began. The body was a woman. They believed she had been in the cistern from six months to two years. A concrete block similar to the ones covering the cistern had been attached to her neck by a piece of cloth.

The police made notes of the body's condition and took special notice of anything that might help them identify her. She was wearing gray pants. She wore three layers on her upper body, including a red cable-knit sweater over a lightweight shirt. Over these she wore a dark pullover shirt.

Two layers of socks covered her feet. On her right and left feet, she wore light-colored, lightweight socks with heavy red socks over them.

Another pair of socks was covering her hands. Rubber bands had been placed over the socks, holding them in place.

The rubber bands seemed so simple but may have been an important clue. Makeshift gloves like these were commonly used by motorcyclists to keep air from going up their sleeves. Since biker groups often gathered at the abandoned property, could she be connected with them? The investigators believed the woman was at least sixty-five years old. Such an advanced age made it hard for the police to believe she was involved with the bikers.

In the cistern, the police also found a bag of items. Among its contents was a key to a Greyhound locker and a memorial key from a revival held by televangelist Jerry Falwell.

The well itself provided few clues. Since the place was used by numerous different groups, from local kids to motorcyclists, in the six months to two years she had been entombed in the cistern, any trace evidence would have been lost.

The mystery of the woman and her death made national and local news. It did not take long for the press to choose a special moniker for the woman. She became known as the Belle in the Well or Belle for short. She would be known by this name for over thirty years.

The Greyhound locker key was one of the first things the police investigated. The employees at the bus station recalled seeing a woman who matched the description of the Belle but did not know her name.

The police believed the Belle had probably been murdered in Huntington, West Virginia. With no specific evidence, this was just a guess.

After an autopsy and further examination, more and more was revealed about the Belle. She was a white female. She appeared to be thirty to sixty years of age. She stood five feet, two inches to five feet, four inches. She had high cheekbones and an overbite. Her lumber and thoracic spine showed evidence of arthritis developing.

The case went cold.

With no way to move the case forward, the Belle needed to have a place to rest. Since her identity was unknown, it was up to Lawrence Countians to pay for her burial. Commissioner Don Lambert donated the land where she was to find peace. Her burial location was left unmarked. This burial would not be her last interment.

Although the Belle's case had grown cold, there were people who still searched for answers. Coroner Bill Nenni tried multiple methods to identify the Belle. Bill had been assigned the case by his father, Coroner Harry Nenni. Bill's attachment to the case caused him to continue to search for answers even after he had officially retired.

In November 2009, the Belle's information was entered into the National Missing and Unidentified Persons System, also known as NamUs. Although the system was unable to identify the Belle, her case caught the attention of forensic anthropologist Elizabeth Murray. Murray contacted Nenni for more information.

On June 15, 2011, the Belle was disinterred. Her remains were X-rayed, and a dental exam was performed. The body was reexamined by the Boyd County, Kentucky coroner's office. They were hoping a new set of eyes might catch something not seen before. Before she was reburied, a three-dimensional facial reconstruction was begun.

DNA was extracted from her molars and sent to NamUs. At the time, it could take up to fourteen months to find matches.

Two different versions of the Belle were released to help identify her. In 2012, the Franklin County, Ohio coroner released the results of the 3D reconstruction. A bust was created from the autopsy photographs. In 2018, the Ohio Bureau of Criminal Investigation created a new 3D facial reconstruction.

In 2013, an updated model of the Belle's face was released by a computer artist.

Four years later, Elizabeth Murray met with a forensic genealogist at a conference. This chance meeting with Colleen Fitzpatrick would open a new path to possibly identifying the Belle. In 2017, Fitzpatrick and Margaret Press joined to form the DNA Doe Project.

The DNA Doe Project was a trailblazing development using investigative genetic genealogy or IGG. A team of volunteers formed to help investigate using genetics and genealogy to solve the identity mysteries of Jane and John Does across the country. The Belle in the Well would be one of the first four cases the project undertook.

Finally, progress was being made. So many methods had been tried to turn Belle from a Jane Doe. There had been many failures, but people were determined to identify her.

Louise Virginia Peterson Flesher.
Author's collection.

A possible identity was found. A woman named Louise Virginia Peterson Flesher had disappeared around November 1979. Born on June 16, 1915, Louise had lived with her mother and grandmother in Fairview, West Virginia, until she was five. Then she lived in Casper, Wyoming, from 1933 to 1942. In 1972, Louise's husband died in Belpre, Ohio. She returned to her roots in West Virginia from 1944 to 1956. She left Parkersburg, West Virginia, in 1956. Next, she lived in Las Vegas, Nevada, until 1979. Her relatives believed she was returning to West Virginia after leaving Las Vegas, but she disappeared. Her relatives learned she was no longer cashing her social security checks but had no way to contact her.

In March 2019, Louise's daughter allowed a DNA mouth swab to be taken.

By July 3, the Belle in the Well had finally been identified. She was Louise Virginia Peterson Flesher.

A conference was held in the Bowman Auditorium at Ohio University Southern to make the announcement. Lawrence County, Ohio coroner Ben Mack was given the honor of speaking to the attendees. The Belle in the Well was no longer a Jane Doe. She had a name. She had a family.

None of Louise's family was among those who attended the conference. They had asked to remain anonymous.

With a verified identity, the case was one step closer to being solved. Forty years had passed since Louise's remains were located in the cistern by the Baxter sisters. Solving a case after so many years will not be easy. However, there is still hope.

Maybe someone reading this book may have the one clue that will finally bring justice to the Belle in the Well, Louise Virginia Peterson Flesher. Any information or tips can be reported using the phone number 740-532-3525 or email helpthesheriff@lawsoco.com.

16

SHOOTING ON THE SHANTY

*S*hanty boats used to be a common sight on the Ohio River. They were a popular way to live from the 1850s to 1950s. Over that century, fifty thousand people would call shanty boats home.

Shanty boat living reached its peak during the Great Depression. At that time, a shanty boat could cost its owner $20 to $30, or around $500 in today's money. If you really wanted a fancy boat, people could spend up to $200 for their new home.

These boats were perfect for those who wanted a low-cost living. They could move along the river to find jobs. Some people even made their livelihood on the river. That is why these boats became so popular in the Great Depression when so many people found themselves homeless. Boat owners often bartered to obtain anything they needed.

The boats consisted of two to three rooms. Their structure and layout were similar to those of shotgun houses.

As time moved on, the shanty boat life began to disappear. The rise in pollution and flooding on the Ohio River contributed to the decline. Floods like the 1937 flood devastated the shanty boats as much as they did the housing and buildings on land.

A particular shanty boat would be the location of a raid and shooting in Lawrence County, Ohio. The shooting ended with more than one power struggle.

On a warm July evening in 1915, six men gathered together in a shanty boat located in a clump of willows. Tied up in front of the Egerton Farm on

WICKED LAWRENCE COUNTY, OHIO

the Ohio shore and across the river from Huntington's Twentieth Street, the boat was a meeting place for men to drink and gamble.

On July 4, 1915, Sheriff Glen Sloan of Proctorville, Ohio, received a phone call informing him of bootleggers and gamblers on a shanty boat. The men had come from nearby Huntington, West Virginia, to enjoy their vices on a shanty boat moored near Proctorville.

Deputy Sheriff Hutchison and Constable Brannigan of Ironton were sent to check out the accusation. Marshal Frank Harmon and two deputies joined them as they made their way to the boat near Chesapeake, Ohio. Later, some questions arose about who was there that Independence Day.

The police found six local men. John "Chink" Chapman, "Rube" Williams, "Dutch" Roach, J.A. Martin and J.A. Chapman, John Chapman's brother, were all from Huntington, West Virginia. A Mr. Spurlock and Mr. Johnson were also present.

When the law officers found the shanty boat moored near Chesapeake, they knew they had the right place. Constable Brannigan was told to remain in the willow trees near the riverbank to catch anyone who tried to flee the scene.

As the officers approached the boat, they saw firsthand evidence of crimes. The six men were gambling. A large stack of poker chips and other gambling paraphernalia was easily visible even from the riverbank.

Stealthily, they approached the boat. They amassed outside the boat's door and demanded entry. The men on the boat claimed Williams opened the door, while the law claimed they had to force their way onto the shanty boat.

Rube Williams was the first person to greet the police and the one who gave the police a fight. He resisted arrest, and Deputy Hutchison had to tackle him to the ground. Most considered Williams the worst of the men present that night, and no one was treating him with kid gloves. Eventually, he was handcuffed and taken into custody.

While Hutchison and William tussled on the shanty's floor, the other men on the boat scattered, each one trying to escape the long arm of the law. Dutch Roach and J.A. Martin ran for the stairs. John Chapman grabbed his coat and ran toward the boat's other door.

Frank Carey, an employee of the Gwinn Flour Company and Chesapeake constable, was one of the men who accompanied the police. He saw Chapman running from the boat. He chased after Chapman. They tore down the gangplank. Halfway down the plank, Carey fired his gun for the first time. A second shot was fired.

Gwinn Flour Company. *Author's collection.*

Those inside the shanty boat heard the shots. The police had captured four of the six men. Williams, Spurlock, Johnson and John's brother were arrested. Upon his return, Carey even slapped the cuffs on Martin and Roach.

According to the police, two men escaped and crossed the river. One of those two men was supposedly John Chapman.

The four men who were captured claimed to be from Huntington, West Virginia. All four were being held in the Chesapeake jail. They would face the court on July 5, 1915.

The events of the evening seemed simple and straightforward. Within days of the raid and arrests, people began to question the official accounting of the night's events.

Although shots had been fired and everyone heard them, the law officers claimed no one had been injured during the raid. Hutchison went on the record stating he had heard the two shots ring out while he was tussling with Williams. When he was asked if anyone was shot, he said no. He was wrong.

John "Chink" Chapman was one of the men who had escaped capture. Only twenty-one years old, he had been there with his brother. Although he would admit to gambling, he had much more to tell when he arrived at B.F. Goodall's house around 1:00 a.m. on July 5. One-fourth of a mile from the shanty boat, it was the first place he sought medical assistance.

Although the police believed everyone had escaped relatively unscathed that night, they were wrong. As John ran away from the shanty boat, two shots were fired. The first shot went through the coat he had so quickly thrown over his arm. Chapman did not stop. He was not going to willingly surrender himself.

The second shot struck him in the shoulder. Carey and John had been only five feet apart when the gun barked a second time.

John lost consciousness from his injuries. He fell off the gangplank and into the weeds at the edge of the Ohio River and disappeared from the officer's sight. John lay among the weeds for several hours before he finally awakened. In pain, he stumbled his way to the nearest safe place he could find.

His first stop was the Goodall house. He was given first aid while notice was sent to Chapman's father. John's father, Augustus Lightburn Chapman, arrived around 2:00 a.m.

Four hours later, John Chapman was taken to his parents' house at 2105 Third Avenue in Huntington, West Virginia. Later, he was taken to Huntington General Hospital, where an operation was performed to remove a revolver ball from just beneath the skin of his right breast.

The wound was described as a clean shot. That did not mean John was not seriously injured. The bullet had smashed his collarbone and shoulder blade. The doctors feared he would lose the use of his shoulder or arm.

John readily admitted he had been gambling with the others on July 4. He, however, firmly claimed he had done nothing deserving of being shot.

Huntington General Hospital. *Author's collection.*

John believed wholeheartedly the police had been shooting to kill. He had just been lucky to survive.

John's father agreed with his son. Augustus was not ignorant of the ways of the police. In fact, Augustus had worked as a police officer in Huntington, West Virginia. As a father, he was not going to allow his concerns to go unanswered.

While his son was recovering in the hospital, Augustus made his way across the river to Chesapeake, Ohio. Angered by his son's injuries, he demanded to know who had shot his son. All law officers denied knowing who had fired the weapon. Augustus was not going to let these sleeping dogs lie. He informed those whom he contacted he would be seeking prosecution for whoever had shot John.

The deputy sheriff from Ironton informed Mr. Chapman of the events of the evening. Chesapeake citizens had called the Lawrence County sheriff Sloan complaining about the Huntington men crossing the river to engage in selling whiskey and running poker games.

On July 4, the sheriff's office had been told the shanty boat contained "a pack of outlaws and thieves." Warrants had been issued for bootlegging. Being warned of the dangerous nature of the men on the boat, the officers were "taking no chances."

Sheriff Sloan had more information to provide Augustus Chapman. He said the police had been misinformed. Further, the sheriff gave the names of the men representing the law in Lawrence County, Ohio, on that night: Deputy Hutchison of Ironton, Deputy Mike Branningan of Ironton, Constable Frank Carey of Chesapeake and Constable Harmon of Chesapeake.

Two of the men arrested on July 4 had already faced arraignment. Dutch Roach, Rube Williams and J.A. Chapman were charged with bootlegging. They each had been released on a two-hundred-dollar bond.

Once released, Dutch Roach and Rube Williams were quick to speak to Augustus about his son's shooting. They identified Frank Carey as the shooter. Based on their testimony, Carey was expected to be arrested.

Even though he was injured, John Chapman would face the court himself on July 7, 1915. He was arrested and given bond. He was to return to court with the other three men.

One question came up that no one was quite expecting. Who had jurisdiction over the prosecution of the shooter? Although the Ohio River shares its name with the state, the State of Ohio does not actually have ownership of the river. The boundary line between West Virginia and

Ohio is the low-water mark on the Ohio shore. Since the shanty boat was in the river, anything that occurred on the boat would fall under West Virginia's jurisdiction.

Oddly, when an arrest was finally made and an indictment was handed down, Constable Carey was not the one chosen to face prosecution. Instead, Deputy Marshal F.M. Harmon was indicted for shooting John Chapman on July 8, 1915. Harmon was arrested on July 9, 1915, by Deputy D.W. Frampton.

Why people suddenly suspected Harmon was not mentioned. Maybe Augustus Chapman's investigation uncovered the truth.

Harmon was arraigned soon after he was arrested. He chose A.J. Layne and John W. Perry of Ironton to represent him. They entered a plea of lack of jurisdiction. Layne and Perry stated Harmon could not face prosecution in West Virginia because the shot was fired in Ohio. Harmon was placed under a thousand-dollar bond and released.

The entire tristate was gearing up for what was going to be one of the most interesting legal battles in the history of Cabell County, West Virginia. The battle was not going to be man against man, but state against state.

Most of the residents of West Virginia sided with the Chapmans. They believed the police had no right to raid the shanty boat, nor should a shot have been fired.

In Ohio, people believed the deputies had been doing their jobs. They were protecting the residents of Chesapeake. They were tired of people coming from West Virginia to break the law in their town.

On July 10, 1915, John Chapman was strong enough to go home. That afternoon, he spent several hours with his parents, August and Virginia "Jennie" Ball. Sadly, he was forced to return to Huntington General Hospital for further treatment under the care of Dr. J.H. Steenbergen.

John Chapman slowly began to recover from his injuries. The recovery was not easy or quick.

On July 21, 1915, John Chapman had a relapse. He was taken back to the hospital, where a second surgery was performed. The bullet had grazed his axillary artery and tore away part of its protective cover. This form of injury caused a weakening of the artery's walls. In its weakened state, the artery had swollen to twice its size.

His health had deteriorated so severely that the doctors could not even state whether or not he would recover. They claimed it would take over forty-eight hours before John's condition improved.

Mount Hope Hospital. *Author's collection.*

The doctors at Mount Hope Hospital denied John's health was deteriorating. They claimed he was recovering nicely from his second surgery on his shoulder.

All of the doctors agreed his arm was far from healed. They could not find any evidence of blood circulating in his arm. With no circulation, his arm would need to be amputated. The question was whether he was capable of surviving the surgery. Apparently, the doctors did not agree on how strong Chapman was.

Since his health was so unsure, three officers went to Chapman's bedside, where they took his statement. While the officers were at the hospital, they were given one of Chapman's broken ribs. The rib was broken by a bullet during the shooting. The broken bone was turned over to the authorities as evidence in the upcoming trial.

Frank Harmon was to be tried on July 28, 1915. For reasons not recorded by the local newspapers, the trial was postponed until November.

In November 1915, Frank Harmon received his day in court. He was officially charged with malicious wounding. Judge T.W. Taylor presided over the case. Since the jurisdiction had been questioned, the judge instructed the jury to place the shooting within the banks of the Ohio River, making Cabell County, West Virginia, the correct place for the case to be heard.

On November 16, 1915, Frank Harmon was found guilty of unlawful shooting. He was sentenced to one year in prison and asked to pay a one-dollar fine.

Former location of the Empire Furniture Company. *Author's collection.*

His attorneys decided that instead of taking the case to a higher court, they would petition Governor Henry Drury Hatfield to pardon Harmon. Even the prosecuting attorney petitioned the governor to grant Harmon a pardon so he would not spend time in prison. In the end, the governor agreed to allow Frank Harmon his freedom.

As for John Chapman, his life moved on. He married Anna McQuithy on October 22, 1927, in Huntington, Cabell County, West Virginia. By the time the 1930 Federal Census was taken, John and Anna had welcomed a little girl named Anna Joe. At first, John worked as a finisher at the Empire Furniture Company, located on the northeast corner of Twenty-Second Street and Second Avenue. Later, he found work at the Huntington Furniture Corporation. John, Anna and their baby girl lived with Augustus and Jennie at 2660 Guyan Avenue.

By 1940, the young Chapman family had moved out of John's parents' home. They had moved into the home of Ashley and Naomi Jones at 727 Sixth Avenue in Huntington as boarders. John continued to work in the furniture factory. Anna had also found a job as a clerk at a bakery.

The 1950 Federal Census shows a few changes to the Chapman household. John and Anna had moved out into their own home at 607 Seventh Avenue.

John continued to work as a finisher at the furniture company. Anna had changed jobs and was working as a pie wrapper at a pie bakery. Anna Joe was no longer living at home with her parents.

On April 20, 1958, John "Chink" Chapman died in Huntington, West Virginia. He was laid to rest in Woodmere Memorial Park in Huntington, West Virginia. Over twenty years later, Anna would be buried beside her husband.

BIBLIOGRAPHY

Red Lights over Lawrence County

Cincinnati (OH) Enquirer. "Ironton." January 23, 1878.
———. "Shepard Is Found Guilty." October 30, 1913.
Ironton (OH) Register. "Common Pleas Court." May 5, 1898.
———. "Common Pleas Court." May 30, 1895.
———. "Common Pleas Court." June 22, 1882.
———. "Jail Rules." April 28, 1898.
———. "Louis L. Halliday." July 4, 1895.
———. "Maggerty." July 8, 1915.
———. "Mayor's Court." March 2, 1876.
Ironton (OH) Tribune. "Ashland Man Arrested at Local Hotel on a White Slavery Charge." July 7, 1915.
Jackson (OH) Standard. "Court of Common Pleas." June 23, 1878.
———. "A Man Named Lawrence Sloan." June 17, 1875.
———. "The Mayor of Ironton…" February 15, 1877.
Morning Irontonian (Ironton, OH). "Lived Here with Woman: Arrested for Violation of White Slave Charge." July 23, 1915.
Semi-Weekly Irontonian (Ironton, OH). "Child Found in House of Bad Repute." May 7, 1907.
———. "Harbored Young Girl." May 7, 1907.
———. "Raided House." November 16, 1915.

Twenty-Second Annual Report of Board of Trustees and Officers of the Athens State Hospital to the Governor of the State of Ohio for the Fiscal Year Ending November 15, 1895. Columbus, Ohio: Westbote Company.

Wilmington (NC) Morning Star. "FBI Raid Breaks Giant White Slave Ring; 49 Persons Held." November 24, 1947.

Continental Nite Club

Beckley (WV) Post-Herald. "Gang 'Clears' Huntington's Ohio Nite Spot." April 27, 1948.

Cincinnati (OH) Enquirer. "Four Clubs Are Hit Bitterly in Bid for EXECUTIVE Power to Pounce." March 13, 1949.

Circleville (OH) Herald. "Mystery Holdup Baffles Police." April 27, 1948.

Cleveland (OH) Magazine. "The Golden Era of the Cleveland Mob." August 1978.

Evening Independent (Massillon, OH). "Lausche Says Club Shut Down." October 24, 1949.

Independent (Long Beach, CA). "L.A.C. Says Supporting Rackets." October 23, 1959.

Ironton (OH) Tribune. "Compressor at Club Lets Go." September 28, 1939.

———. "Governor Lausche Orders County 'Clean Up.'" August 9, 1945.

———. "Lausche New Ohio Governor." January 10, 1949.

Jacksonville (IL) Daily. "Cleveland 'Boss' Made Thousands in Steel Merger." March 1, 1951.

Lancaster Eagle-Gazette. "Fire Opened in War Against Gambling by Officials in Several Ohio Counties." March 15, 1949.

———. "Plan Small Shopping Center at Gallipolis." December 2, 1960.

Mansfield (OH) News-Journal. "Ohio Counties Crack Down on Gambling." March 15, 1949.

Marion (OH) Star. "Four More Change Gambling Pleas." March 15, 1949.

Martin, Martha Kounse. "The Continental Club." *Lawrence Register*, accessed August 20, 2023. https://lawrencecountyohio.com.

News-Journal (Mansfield, OH). "Openly Condemns 4 'Clubs.'" March 13, 1949.

Portsmouth (OH) Daily Times. "Sues for Damages." September 25, 1941.

Sandusky (OH) Register. "Jungle Inn Raze Order Is Reversed." January 4, 1951.

———. "Lausche Charter Says Casino Not Charitable as Instituted." March 7, 1950.
Stanberry (MO) Herald-Headlight. "Nevada Gambling Aids Underworld." November 12, 1959.
Times Recorder (Zanesville, OH). "Pettibone Club to Be Closed." May 23, 1946.

Sister-in-Law from Hell

Ironton (OH) Register. "Lawrence County in the Penitentiary." May 27, 1869.
———. "Murder at Mount Vernon." April 30, 1863.
Portsmouth (OH) Times. "Murder." May 2, 1863.

Crimes of the Innocent

BG News (Bowling Green State University). "Couple to Be Sentenced Bread and Water." November 14, 1979.
Daily Kent Stater (Kent, OH). "Bread-and-Water Jail Sentence Rescinded." November 15, 1979.
Defiance (OH) Crescent News. "Judge Agrees Not to Lock Up Youth." April 27, 1982.
Dover (OH) Times Reporter. "Without After-Care, New Laws Won't Work, OYC's Willis Says." August 28, 1981.
Ironton (OH) Tribune. "Burwell to Order Record Microfilming." June 13, 1980.
———. "Former Judge Left Mark." October 3, 1995.
———. "Obituary: Lloyd Burwell." October 3, 1995.
Logan (OH) Daily News. "Appointments by Rhodes." December 21, 1976.
Mansfield (OH) News. "2 Officials Jailed for Short Time." March 8, 1977.
Norwalk (OH) Reflector. "Judge Tough on Truants." January 17, 1978.
Portsmouth (OH) Times. "Burwell to Seek Office of Prosecutor." December 1, 1959.
———. "Scout Executive Resigning: New Director Sought." September 17, 1970.
———. "Siple Loses in Lawrence County." November 10, 1960.
Washington Court House (OH) Record Herald. "Appeals Court Frees Two Commissioners." March 8, 1977.

Charles Shafer: Husband, Father, Murderer

Cincinnati (OH) Enquirer. "Cornered Shafer Killed Himself." June 15, 1907.
Ironton (OH) Tribune. "Court of Common Pleas." June 14, 1906.
———. "Shafer Tragedy." June 20, 1907.
Raleigh Herald (Beckley, WV). "Most Fiendish of Murders Slays with Shotgun." June 20, 1907.
Shenandoah Herald (Woodstock, VA). "Triple Murdered Commits Suicide." June 21, 1907.
Washington Post (Washington, D.C.). "Suicide to Evade Capture." June 15, 1907.

From Freedom to Slavery: The Polley Kidnapping Case

Anti-Slavery Bugle (Lisbon, OH). "Peyton Polley Case." January 10, 1852.
Atlas of Lawrence County, Ohio: Hardesty–1882, Lake–1887. Lawrence County Genealogical Society, 1985.
Ellis, Atiba R. "Polley v. Ratliff: A New Way to Address on Original Sin?" *West Virginia University Law Review* (December 2012).
Hall, James L. "The Famous Negro Polley Family of Lawrence County, Part 1." *Herald Dispatch* (Huntington, WV), October 9, 2014.
Herald Dispatch (Huntington, WV). "The Famous Polley Family of Lawrence County, Part 3." October 23, 2014.
Ironton (OH) Register. "Called on Lincoln." July 11, 1895.
Ironton (OH) Weekly Register. "Obituary: Hon. Ralph Leete." July 20, 1905.
Spirit of the Times (Ironton, OH). "It Will Be Remembered…" March 22, 1853.
———. "The Polley Kidnapping Case." June 6, 1854.

The Mysterious Death of Avanelle Smith

Daily Reporter (Dover, OH). "Woman's Body Found." May 13, 1863.
Evening Review (East Liverpool, OH). "Woman's Body Found in Ravine Identified." May 14, 1963.
Ironton (OH) Tribune. "May Grand Jury Reports." May 22, 1963.
———. "Probe Continuing in Woman's Death." May 17, 1963.
———. "Proctorville Woman Identified in Probe." May 14, 1963.

———. "Woman's Body Discovered in Ravine." May 12, 1963.
———. "Woman's Death Remains Mystery." May 14, 1963.
Lancaster (OH) Eagle. "Identify Body of Woman Found Near Ironton." May 14, 1963.
Sandusky (OH) Register. "FBI Probes Ohio Death." May 17, 1963.

All for Love: Dueling Women

Ancestry. Ohio, U.S., County Marriage Records, 1774–1993. Ancestry.com.
———. West Virginia, U.S., Births Index, 1804–1938. Ancestry.com.
Cincinnati (OH) Enquirer. "Sunday Night Struggles on the Road." May 23, 1889.
Ironton (OH) Register. "The Girl Fight." May 30, 1889.
Pittsburgh (PA) Post. "Girls Fight a Duel." May 23, 1889.
Summit County Beacon (Akron, OH). "At Athalia." May 29, 1889.

The Safecrackers

Ironton (OH) Register. "Hides Their Faces." June 13, 1889.
———. "Prisoners Sentenced." June 20, 1889.
———. "Safe-Blowing." May 29, 1889.

Ballard Robbers

Ironton (OH) Register. "Court of Common Pleas." March 4, 1869.
———. "Court of Common Pleas." May 20, 1869.
———. "Court of Common Pleas." May 27, 1869.
———. "Gone to Penitentiary." June 3, 1869.
———. "Ike Ballard Arrested." October 22, 1868.
———. "In Jail." October 22, 1868.
———. "A Visit to the Jail." February 25, 1869.
Lamkin, Uel W. *History of Henry County, Missouri.* United States: Historical Publishing Company, 1919.

Badger Game

Chillicothe (OH) Gazette. "Badger Game Outfit All Tinctured with Crime." November 16, 1915.
———. "A Glimpse Over the Annals of the Year." December 31, 1915.
———. "Inquiries About the Patterson Girl." November 22, 1915.
———. "Mrs. Patterson Will Hike on Way Out of City." November 30, 1915.
———. "Mystery of Means of Existence of Strange Trio About to be Solved." November 15, 1915.
———. "101 Ranch Will be Here Tomorrow." September 10, 1913.
———. "Susie Patterson Under Arrest in Chillicothe." November 19, 1915.
———. "Think Patterson Woman Involved in U.S. Case." December 2, 1915.

Bowman versus Stapleton

Baltimore (MD) Sun. "Joseph Stapleton and Milton Bowman…" April 3, 1880.
Cincinnati (OH) Enquirer. "Ironton, Ohio." April 3, 1880.
———. "Ironton, Ohio." April 6, 1880.
Daily Gazette (Wilmington, DE). "Fatal Cutting Affray." April 3, 1880.
Ironton (OH) Register. "Vicious Assault." April 8, 1880.
Ironton (OH) Tribune. "Death." January 6, 1881.
Jackson (OH) Standard. "Joseph Stapleton and Milton Bowman…" April 15, 1880.
National Republican (Washington, D.C.). "Killed His Brother-In-Law." April 3, 1880.
Somerset (OH) Press. "A Post Mortem…" April 15, 1880.

Femme Fatale: The Story of Nancy Patterson Moreland

Ironton (OH) Evening Tribune. "Mystery Veils 'Charmer's Death." October 31, 1933.
———. "New Version Develops in Murder Case." October 29, 1933.
———. "Porter Improving; Moreland Rites Today; No Legal Action Yet Taken." October 31, 1933.

———. "Porter-Moreland Inquest Set for Next Wednesday." November 1, 1933.

Ironton (OH) Tribune. "Arraignment of Moreland on Shooting Charge Is Postponed." January 15, 1928.

———. "Bartram Gives Self Up: In Jail." July 28, 1933.

———. "Bartram Released on Bond." July 31, 1933.

———. "Bartram Rites Next Friday." February 1, 1928.

———. "Bartram to Enter His Plea Today." July 28, 1933.

———. "Bartram Will Be Arraigned Monday." July 30, 1933.

———. "Bond on First Degree Murder Charge Cause of Controversy." July 31, 1933.

———. "Moreland's Widow Files Charges Against Bartram." July 27, 1933.

———. "Much Speculation as to Official Steps in Attorney's Case." October 31, 1933.

———. "Obituary: Bartram." February 3, 1928.

———. "Physicians Fight to Save Life of Prosecuting Attorney Porter." October 30, 1933.

———. "Porter Bought Gun Used in Slaying Woman." October 29, 1933.

———. "Porter's Conduct Has Been Quite Peculiar." October 30, 1933.

———. "South Side Gas Station Robbed: Bartram at Large." July 26, 1933.

———. "Stanley Bartram Shot by Herman Moreland." January 12, 1928.

———. "Victim of Gun Fight Has Chance for Life." January 13, 1928.

———. "Victim of Recent Gun Fight Died at Home This Morning." January 31, 1928.

———. "Victim Shot Down During Card Game at Eagle Hall Here." July 26, 1933.

Sandusky (OH) Register. "Ironton Prosecutor Shot by Widow Who Then Takes Own Life." October 29, 1933.

Murder on Tick Ridge

Coshocton (OH) Democrat. "Two Brothers Die in Ohio Gun Fight." March 19, 1956.

Daily Reporter (Dover, OH). "Still Found Near Scene of Shooting." March 21, 1956.

Evening Review (East Liverpool, OH). "Ohioan Found Guilty in Gun Slayings." June 18, 1956.

Ironton (OH) Tribune. "Dave Daniels Charged with Murder of Two." March 27, 1956.

———. "David Daniels." March 19, 1956.

———. "David Daniels Admits Shooting Two Larges." March 19, 1956.

———. "David Daniels Found Guilty of Second Degree Murder." June 17, 1956.

———. "Full Measure of Slayings." March 20, 1956.

———. "Grand Jury Nears End of Session." March 23, 1956.

———. "Grand Jury Will Return Thursday." March 19, 1956.

———. "Large Case Not Ready for Jury." March 22, 1956.

———. "Motive for Murder?" March 20, 1956.

———. "Murder Inquiry Postpones Jury." March 19, 1956.

———. "Obituaries." March 22, 1956.

———. "Spears Expects to File Charges Thursday." March 19, 1956.

———. "Still May Be Linked In Shooting of Larges." March 20, 1956.

Lancaster (OH) Eagle-Gazette. "Still Found Near House in Which Brothers Slain." March 20, 1956.

Logan (OH) Daily News. "Moonshine Still Linked to Slayings." March 20, 1956.

Marysville (OH) Journal-Tribune. "Two Brothers Shot to Death in Family Battle." March 20, 1956.

Times Recorder (Zanesville, OH). "Found Guilty on Two Murders Counts." June 18, 1956.

The Belle in the Well

Ironton (OH) Tribune. "Being Named at Last." July 31, 2019.

Shaffer, Mark. "'Belle in the Well' Name Revealed." *Ironton (OH) Tribune,* July 30, 2019.

———. "Belle's DNA Leads to Name History." *Ironton (OH) Tribune,* July 30, 2019.

Zhang, Sarah. "She Was Found Strangled in a Well and Now She Has a Name." *The Atlantic,* July 29, 2019.

Shooting on the Shanty

Ironton (OH) Register. "Boat Gamblers Are Arrested." July 5, 1915.
———. "Chesapeake Officer Is Indicted at Huntington." July 8, 1915.
———. "Indict Harmon for Shooting Chapman in Gambling Raid." July 9, 1915.
———. "Local Officers Give Version of Shooting Affray at Proctorville." July 7, 1915.
———. "Man Shot When Officers Raid Boat." July 7, 1915.
Morning Irontonian (Ironton, OH). "Chapman Able to Go to His Home to See Parents." July 11, 1915.
———. "Chapman May Die As Result of Wounds." July 21, 1915.
———. "Chapman's Wound Had Healed Too Rapidly." July 22, 1915.
———. "Will Claim Harmon Was in Ohio at Time the Shot Was Fired." July 10, 1915.

General Resources

Ancestry. Appointments of U.S. Postmasters, 1832–1971. Ancestry.com.
———. 1850 United States Federal Census. Ancestry.com.
———. 1860 United States Federal Census. Ancestry.com.
———. 1870 United States Federal Census. Ancestry.com.
———. Ohio, U.S., Births and Christenings Index, 1774–1973. Ancestry.com.
———. Ohio, U.S., County Marriage Records, 1774–1993. Ancestry.com.
———. 1900 United States Federal Census. Ancestry.com.
———. 1910 United States Federal Census. Ancestry.com.
———. 1920 United States Federal Census. Ancestry.com.
———. 1930 United States Federal Census. Ancestry.com.
———. 1940 United States Federal Census. Ancestry.com.
———. 1950 United States Federal Census. Ancestry.com.
Ancestry and The Church of Jesus Christ of Latter-day Saints. 1880 United States Federal Census. Ancestry.com.

ABOUT THE AUTHOR

*L*ori Shafer was born and raised in Lawrence County, Ohio. A graduate of the Ironton City Schools, she became interested in history at an early age. Family vacations to historical sites in the tristate area only increased her desire to learn about the history of the world around her. Once she began working at Briggs Lawrence County Public Library, she was motivated to discover more about the diverse history of Lawrence County, Ohio. Her first book, *Iron Furnaces of Lawrence County, Ohio*, was published in 2009. Since then, she has published six others, including a revision of her first book. Her primary focus has been preserving local history and enticing people to learn about local history.

Visit us at
www.historypress.com
....